An Obscure Life

Things I never wanted to talk about

An Obscure Life

Things I never wanted to talk about

ROBERT FORGE

ARPress
ILLUMINATING IDEAS
EMPOWERING VOICES

ARPress
45 Dan Road Suite 5
Canton MA 02021

Hotline: 1(888) 821-0229
Fax: 1(508) 545-7580

Ordering Information:
Quantity sales.Special discounts are available on quantity purchases by corporations, associations, and others.For details, contact the publisher at the address above.

Printed in the United States of America.

ISBN-13:   Paperback   979-8-89389-211-6
                  eBook   979-8-89389-212-3

Library of Congress Control Number: 2024905651

Table Of Contents

Prologue

I cannot believe that I attempted to even write a book never mind about myself and stories that I never wanted to tell everyone. I was never a book reader to begin with and when I did, I would get sleepy every time. Some of the stories in here I have told people over the years with mixed results back. You're crazy or you must have dreamt that. Where you high at the time? Or the classic, get outta here. Some years I was all of that, but not when I wrote this. The stories are real and not some figment of my imagination. My long-term memory is sharp but sometimes I will walk into a room and forget what I went in there for. It's as if the thought leaked out of my ears and vanished in thin air.

The real reason for this burst of remembrances is for my family to really know who I was and who I had become, especially my grandchildren. I know they are being brought up right and will be people of good character one day as they are being raised to high and moral standards. Thank God, they will not have to follow my path and life of hard knocks because of their mother and father. I love them all. And my wife of almost 40 years is the best grandmother there is.

Also, by writing this it has become a therapeutic tool for myself to step back and reflect on the struggles and triumphs in my life and, overcome and deal with the bad within. The book's title can be used as a verb or adjective. I use it as an adjective as in vague or unknown. So please do not judge me harshly and enjoy the story of **An Obscure Life.**

Chapter 1
Early Years

Dec.22 1951

Born on December 22, 1951, at Cambridge City Hospital, Cambridge Massachusetts. My earliest memory was around three years old. I remember sitting in my highchair and my grandmother was feeding me spaghetti. Then I picked it up with my fingers and smeared it on my face and got some in my mouth. I remember grandma laughing about this to my mother. My mother and my uncle Al (known as Uncle Lolly) all lived in the same apartment on Putnam Ave in Cambridge. This was a three-story wood framed building with three apartments left and right. We lived on the first floor left. Uncle Lolly was a lonely man that spent most of his time in his room off the kitchen. He worked at a bicycle shop repairing them as long as I had known him. He had a fascination with magnets and had quite a few as I remember at around age five. He used some to prop open his bedroom door sometimes.

He also loved Mad magazine and kept them all. Uncle Lolly was a very caring person and I loved him very much. He was my guardian angel.

Uncle and I would sit in the living room on two kitchen chairs, so we were close to the little TV. We would watch Behind the Green Door (spooky) and Howdy Doody for me. We spent a lot of time together in front of the TV. I was only 5 years old when he moved out and it broke my heart. There was no explanation as to why he left, but I would not have understood anyway at my age.

I was left alone to fend for myself much of the time after that. And I had no idea where my grandmother was and there wasn't anyone to check in on me. Just me and my mother and she was not around much.

She never had a job that I know of, she was either in a bar drinking with friends or who knows where. Sometimes she would bring me along as her and her friends would drink and blow smoke around me. Back in that era drinking and smoking was advertised to be healthy for you. Mother was rarely home, and I was hungry most of the time and made myself sandwiches A piece of bread with sugar on top, and sometimes ate pictures of food that I saw in magazines. Survival in its worst form and I did not know any other way being so young. I didn't venture outside much because I was afraid and lived in a tough neighborhood near the railroad tracks on one side and some brick apartments on the other with wild, crazy kids that would pick on me. One time I got fed up with this one boy that bullied me, and I got up above him and dropped a brick on his head and he started bleeding. He went off crying and never bothered me again.

I remember that Uncle Lolly left his old Plymouth alongside the building a lot of the time. It did not run, and I sat in it a lot just playing. Pretending to drive away to somewhere better I thought.

The toilet that had an overhead tank and a pull chain. Also, an old stove that you could put wood in and burn it for heat in the kitchen, or so it seemed. My mother and I had a bedroom together with twin beds when she was there. I slept alone most nights as I remember.

Alone and scared.

Like I said she was always out somewhere and when my uncle wasn't there he was at work. When he was, he looked after me.

There was a statue of Jesus on the bureau that was fascinating to me, and I did look at it quite a bit as I passed through the room, not sure who he was. One night alone I was awakened by the beautiful image of Jesus next to my bed. He looked like the statue. I must have been in bad health or something, why would he present himself to me? He talked to me and made hand gestures as if he were blessing me. I could not tell you what was said. Then he glided across the floor and vanished thru the closet door and into it. I got up and went to look for him right away. Normally I was too scared of the dark closet, but I felt at peace and wanted more of his company. I am not afraid of dying to

this day, as I know what awaits me. *I hope.* I feel blessed by this. My memory of this is clear to this day and I am not trying to remember a dream. He was with me. Things for me changed after that encounter and my uncle came back in my life to care for me.

At some point in life me and my mother moved to Pine Street near Central Sq. after a short stay at some homeless shelter or something by the Charles River (Lots of older people there and I remember getting stung by a wasp.) Anyway, I walked along the Charles River many times to get out of the creepy homeless shelter and would run across a gang of bullies a couple of times and they would talk bad and push me down a lot, but I had to take it or get a good beating. Three against one.

The apartment was a two-story wood framed building with four units. I had a closet like room next to my mother's bedroom that I slept in. They were building another like it right behind ours. This became my first curiosity with construction. I loved watching the progress and playing with the lumber making bridges and odd things on the weekend when they had the time off. I spent many hours by myself totally adsorbed with my new obsession. Little did I know later in life this would become my occupation. Carpenter.

Then I met Rippy, an overweight black kid who lived across the street with his mother and sister on the 3rd floor of his building. We became close friends, and we would make water balloons and throw them out of the window at cars until his mother caught us. We did not mess with big momma and didn't do that again. We would ride our bicycles around the area and one day I saw Rippy run into the front of a car that was turning the corner. He landed on the hood and that man was mad because he made a dent being so overweight. He walked his bike home not hurt, other than his pride.

There was a corner grocery store with apartments above and around the back of them in the evening bats would come out from the roof somewhere and scare everyone. Kids would hold their mothers fur coats or fuzzy things on a stick as high as they could, and the bats would circle around them. The little girls would scream. I thought that was so funny, He He. Good times I say.

Rippy's mom was a very caring woman and tried to have me removed from my mother due to the deplorable conditions that I lived in. I slept with lots of cockroaches each night and was full of bites. Sometimes she would take me to dinner with her family. I was an embarrassment I'm sure, but she felt sad for me I guess and didn't care what people thought about this as we ate in silence at a restaurant. Yes, as usual, I was hungry, dirty, smelly etc. I would sometimes walk to this old women's house down the street, and she would give me fruit and whatever she had left over and complain about my mother not feeding me. Nothing ever changed from it.

Around the corner from the apartments was a supply yard that had piles of slate shingles for roofs. There was a chain link fence around it with many sections missing. I remember my friends and I would play hide and seek around the piles of slate. One time I was playing there by myself jumping from one pile to another and saw a horizontal pipe with no fence attached to it and decided to jump and grab it. I missed and my life went into slow motion, there were many sharp edges of slate sticking up that I was looking at and heading for. This was going to be awfully bad. I landed softly on it as if someone slowly put me down. Not even a scratch. I thought Jesus saved me again.

I continued being unsupervised during the day and doing every stupid kid trick I could think of. I watched superman on the tube a lot and thought I could lift the corner of a car. I tried and ended up with a hernia operation. Stupid kid stuff again. One time I drank red cool aid and laid down in the street and let it dribble from my mouth. One of the kids went and told my mother to look out the window. She did, and I heard a loud scream from the window and then again, when I went inside. She wasn't happy with me about my side show. It is one of the only times I remember her caring enough to have a reaction at all.

Again, I still did not know where my uncle was, and I missed him. My mother was in her prime at this location with her best friend Gerry (a woman) living next door. They would communicate a lot by going into the bathroom, open the medicine cabinets, and speak thru the vent hole in the back of it as they were back-to-back cabinets.

4

Apartment on Pine St.

Mother had many friends, men, and woman and one morning when I got up, there was a man that was screwing a woman on the coach as I walked through to the kitchen where my mom and Gerry were sitting and watching as if waiting their turn or something. I was seven. How could a mother ever let a child see stuff like that? Mother would sometimes hire a babysitter to keep me in at night; she was 13 and wanted to experiment with touching my private parts. I guess that I was curious as well and we did things everywhere we could be alone. Even in the basement. Just touching, I think.

Sometime during all this, Uncle Lolly returned to my life once again. He brought me a bike and taught me how to ride it in front of the school yard along the black iron fence. I crashed into it a couple of times but learned quickly as I had enough bruising from the fence. Uncle Lolly got his car running again and took us all to my aunt Lorraine's house out of town in Billerica, Mass. It wasn't too far from Cambridge. My aunt, her husband Bill, my cousin Bill JR. and my cousin Annette all lived in a new home in a new neighborhood still being developed.

5

Uncle Lolly parked his car in the sloped driveway and at the end, there was telephone pole across the driveway as a tire stop. Well, I got in the car and somehow put it in neutral. I went rolling past the back of the house and porch where everyone was congregating including my grandmother. The car bumped over the pole and headfirst off the edge of the driveway, the car landed dead center on a huge boulder below, and I started crying. A construction worker scaled the rock and pulled me out of the car. My poor grandmother had some heart problems back then and me rolling by didn't help. I never saw her again. Not sure if I was responsible or not to this day if she had a heart attack or something. We never saw Uncle Lolly's car again either.

I do remember chocking on some hard candy in my aunt's house and they couldn't extract it, so my aunt held me upside down and banged my head on the floor a few times and out it came. Ouch.

Sometime soon after all that, we moved to Cherry St. one street over and parallel to Pine St. this was a 3-story wood frame apartment building, one apartment per floor. We were on the bottom. These apartments went from front to back of building so you could get airflow in the warm months. There wasn't any A/C in the apartment at that time. I went to a catholic school blocks away. That didn't go well because I had no discipline in my life and got in trouble a lot. I think I was almost eight and just started 1st grade.

My mother could not afford the uniforms and the nuns would piecemeal parts of used uniforms for me. I was definitely a standout in a crowd. Always in need of bath and clean clothes. One day I took a paper clip and a rubber band and hit the nun in the back of the head with it. That brought on the dreaded spanking machine she said was in the closet. No one had ever been to the dreaded spanking machine before me. I was pulled in there and you could hear a pin drop and see the fear in their eyes as if I would not come out alive. Well, I came out looking confused and smiling but alive and not hurt. I didn't finish first grade at that school. I think they asked for me to leave. Bad example or something and transferred to a parochial school closer to where I lived.

On the corner of Cherry St was a laundry with an old Chinese man that ran it. For some unknown reason we would sneak up on the window and look at the old man then we would rub our teeth sideways with our fingers at him. This was some sort of insult or something he didn't like. One day when we tried that, he was ready and came running out with a sword and chased us down the street. My friends never ran so fast as they passed by me. I started first grade again at the Robert's School (really), but they moved me up to 2nd grade soon after. I guess I learned something from the nuns.

Robert's School, the name changed later.

Nothing changed with my mother on Cherry St. I remember dragging her into the apartment from the hall after seeing her drunk on her back with her dress up for all to see. I pulled her dress down and dragged her to the bed.

My uncle Lolly would come by with his whiskey to watch TV and me in the evening. In the summer months we had to leave the windows

7

open and people on the streets would stick their heads in the window and my uncle would chase them away.

There was a Welch's candy factory near Central Sq. and one Sunday me and my buddies found a trailer backed up to the dock with the back door unlocked. Yreka. The mother lode of chocolate covered cherries and so much more. Every kid on the street had candy for eternity it seemed like. We would bring the covered cherries to the overpass and throw them at passing cars. That upset a lot of drivers and we would leave before the cops came. Being around 1959, we had vendors on bicycles with a grinding wheel in front of the handlebars for sharpening kitchen knives, fruit vendors with horse drawn wagons yelling to everyone around. When you wanted coal for the furnace, you put a sign in the window, and they would dump it into the basement thru the little window. If you needed ice for the fridge, you put the sign out "This was an era of crime for me" The chocolates set me off because it was easy picking. Next thing you know I was stealing Jimmy Fund donation cans from store counters for the money. This was for crippled kids with polio. I just needed to eat. I lived close to Harvard University and went there to steal purses. The popular thing for students was to ride 3 speed Raleigh bicycles with the wire baskets on each side of the rear wheel. The girls would always put their purses in them. Easy picking again. They never knew what happened, as I was a young blooming criminal. I don't recall what else other than just stealing stuff when I could. Simply basic survival in the big city to me.

Uncle Lolly got a room around the corner from Pine Street, and I would go by there to visit and look at MAD magazine and he would give me a quarter so I could get into the Boston Museum of Science. I would then head off to the subway station, get on top above the entry turnstiles and get between the overhead signs and come down inside. Then I would slide through the metal bars as I was so skinny and avoid the token turnstiles and wait. People would look at me and never say a word. They could tell by my appearance what I was, *desperate*.

Then I would get off the train on the Boston side and walk to the museum, pay my 25 cents, and enter the most fascinating world of mystery and knowledge a boy could ever imagine. I absorbed many

hours each day as I went looking and learning everything there was to see. I learned about electricity, insects, and snakes that they let you handle, and astronomy. I remember the giant fly exhibit and studied that thing a lot with the eyes and hairs that was bigger than real life as you normally see on one. The museum is still a strong memory to this day and the best experience of my young life. I finally found something good and meaningful that would turn my life around.

Somewhere along life's journey, I became a big brother to David, Loretta, Loraine, and a baby named Mark. I don't remember them being born, they just seemed to come out of nowhere. Mother called the two girls Twinkie and Pruny for fun. I did my best to care for them when mother wasn't around, and sadly baby Mark died after a year or so later. He was very sick and cried a lot. My brother and two sisters would look out the front window like the curious children they were and chew on the wood sill, this was full of lead paint, which is what was used back then. I still blame the lead paint for my brother's learning disability's he never got over. On the other hand, maybe they were probably hungry like me. Mother always had a big pot of lard on the stove, and I would heat this up, peel potatoes and make French fries for us. That's all I knew how to cook. Oh, and toast. Usually, the stale bread that the roaches helped themselves to. When she was around, she would do the laundry and make better food. At Christmas she did put up an aluminum tree with the light wheel that would change the color constantly. We loved it though. Sometimes we would go and look for a real Christmas tree and I would drag it back and help decorate it. And we had a train set that circled the tree. She did have some concern and care for us, but I think the alcoholism turned her into a person of disinterest or confusion. After all she was only in her mid 20's about this time. Then one morning as I was standing in line to enter the school, I heard my name being called. Bobby, Bobby, and I turned around to see a man on the other side of the tall black iron fence looking at me. He asked if I was Bobby.

I said "yes" and he said I need to talk to you. I was very apprehensive at first because of all the perverts that tried to lure me in around the neighborhood, but I went over there because I felt a genuine connection with this man. This seemed different. He said, I'm your father and

I want to get you out of school today and bring you back to your mother's apartment with her to talk. He did, they did talk, and they left for several hours. He brought me a Radio Flyer red wagon, as a peace offering, I guess. Very popular brand in those days. I curled up in it all night and remember them coming back late that night. I was watching some late show as he held her up when they came through the door, drunk of course, put her to bed and said I want to take you with me Bobby, you will have a better life. I said no I want to stay here. He left and soon after knocked on the glass of the front window. I opened it and he said please come with me. He tried to lift me out and I said,

"Not without my wagon".

I got the wagon and never saw my mother again or heard anything about her until I was in Texas many years later and my aunt Lorraine called and said she had passed away from throat cancer and was buried in a cemetery in Fitchburg Mass.

(Enough said, I'm crying)

Chapter 2
A New Beginning

I was taken to a town called Greenwich in Connecticut. (Now a place for the rich and famous) and to a small home about a block from the lake. My father was on another power plant job nearby. I had a yard and would make teepees from fallen branches just like I saw at the museum of science. I was given some old blankets to wrap around it and spent many hours alone playing games and pretending the bad guys were coming or acting like an Indian in a teepee alone. There also was a woman and her teenage daughter living there. His girlfriend's name was Stinky after the tattoo of a skunk she had on her arm. Dad had plenty of tattoos also from his time in the Navy. The strange thing was there was only two bedrooms and me and the daughter (Alice) would have to sleep together. When she came in later at night, I would peek at her getting changed to catch a glimpse of her ample booby's. I liked this arrangement, but she complained about me looking. I was told to roll over when she came in. The nerve of her.

I did have to catch a school bus and that was a new thing for me and had to adjust to the ribbing being the new kid and all. It didn't take long for me to make new friends. There was not any stealing going on here, not a store or university in sight. Luckily, I had changed my ways. I wasn't that great with math homework and Dad used flash cards to help me with division math. Every time I gave a wrong answer, I got a swat across the face. I learned it fast. What a concept.

There was one time in the winter when the lake froze over and me and my friends all stood on the ice and opened our coats to catch the wind and slid across the lake about a half mile to the other side without thinking how we were going to get back. One of my friends went to a house and called his parents to come get us. They were not

happy about this stunt that we did, and I never said a word to my father. I didn't want another swat across the face. Usually though if I was doing adult like things, he didn't care and would laugh it off if it wasn't wimpy kid stuff. Otherwise, a scolding and a grow up son speech. We did not live there for long as my father's job was working on building power plants for generating electricity. After that job, we moved to Thomaston, Ct. to another home where I had my own bedroom. (Don't know what happened to Alice) genuinely nice small community and very hilly. In the winter, my dad would go sledding with me sometimes on a hill right next door. In the summer I learned about licking the syrup from the white honey suckle flowers from the kids in the neighborhood. A wonderful natural sweetness. I had a friend named Patty that lived three houses down, we were both 9 yrs. old. We would sometimes go up this hill behind our homes in the cow pasture behind a hump and learn to kiss. This was good a few times until the farmer on his tractor saw us and fired his shotgun in the air to scare us off. We didn't do that again, but we would still kiss in her game room in the basement sometimes.

I learned how to mow grass then and it was a bitch going up the steep incline of the front yard with a push mower. I don't mean gas powered either. Then the winters when the plows covered up the sidewalks with snow and I had to walk in the street to school with the traffic zooming by. And yes, it was a good mile or more. (Uphill both ways) he he. You kids these days are too soft. My dad bought me a bow and arrow set and I really took to it. Practiced a lot in the big yard we had. In addition, my school had an archery class, and I became a bit of a showoff. I had a dog named Woody because we got him in Woodbridge Ct. Woody was my best friend and constant companion. I would play on the floor in the living room at night with my plastic building blocks and built so many homes or architectural oddities as Dad and Stinky would watch TV. This set had windows and doors also roof parts. Dad and Stinky were amazed at how well I did with this. One thing I did learn from her was the proper way to use utensils, how to set the table and turn your knife blade towards you on the edge of the plate. What I really hated was the fact there was always a serving of beets with dinner once a week and they made me

eat this misconception of fine dining. The beet juice would run into the mashed potatoes and make them taste like beets. I argued constantly about this and was told to shut up and eat it. So, I ate the stupid beets and beet tasting potatoes from the juice first to get the taste out of my mouth so I could enjoy the rest of my meal. When she wasn't in my life anymore, I never touched a beet again to this day and would die first if it was the last food on earth.

There was a period that my dad went into the attic on weekends for hours over several weeks and I was strictly forbidden to go up there. Then one Christmas morning he said go look in the attic, there is something up there for you. When I opened the door there was a special sweater that I could only use when I went up there in the frigid winter months. I walked up and I saw a miracle. The most beautiful train set in the world. Two pieces of plywood laid end to end at table height with a city, a bridge, and tunnels then Cape Canaveral and rockets and cars, people, railroad crossings and coffee grounds along the tracks to look like gravel. This couldn't possibly be mine. It must be an exhibit not to be touched. Then he showed me how to use it and before long, I had to be told many times to come down from there before I froze to death. When I was in the attic, I was in my own world up there. Sometimes I would bring my dog Woody up there with me and would get his nose in the way and derail the train. I had to leave him downstairs from there on. Goofy dog.

Summer came along and I was brought out to Pennsylvania somewhere for a couple of months and lived with some relatives of Stinky's. This was very cool because the family had a traveling carnival. I was shown how to take tickets and start the ride and watch the children go around in a circle in the little cars that mimicked the real ones. When I was not taking tickets, I would ride the spinning chairs that swung out further on the chains the faster it went around. Sometimes we would entertain ourselves by picking up a low voltage wire on the ground that had a bare wire in the length that was used to run the lights and we would join hands and get a shock. Of course, they put me on the end to watch me shake as I was shocked, and the last person got the worst of it. Everyone had a good laugh. I remember sitting on the front porch at their house one morning and counted the number of railroad coal cars that passed by in the distance hillside and stopped counting in the hundreds somewhere. Coal was still the main energy source for this country back then. I still don't understand how that much weight can be pulled without the wheels of the locomotive slipping.

Summer came to an end and Dad, Stinky and I ended up in New London, Ct. We had a 3rd floor apartment this time across the Thames River from the submarine base. And next to the Coast Guard Academy. I watched the subs come in and out of the base as I walked to school and back past the Coast Guard Academy. It was two blocks down the street, and I had to walk past the front and parade grounds each day. I enjoyed watching the cadets march in formation on the weekends. They all looked so clean and perfect in their bright white uniforms. The biggest thrill was seeing the submarines come up and down the river each day. Then on the way out to sea they would pass under the bridge next to the elementary school I went too and out to the Atlantic Ocean.

The Coast Guard Academy / New London, Conn.

14

My dad got me hooked up with a paper route and I had to get up each morning at 5:00 and go pick up the papers with my red wagon (a new one) and deliver them. Then before school, I had to wash the dishes from the night before. This just wasn't right since the stinker was there all day. I guess they thought this was good discipline to learn. Child slavery I thought. I slept on a cot in the dining room and sometimes read Hardy Boys books about their life of adventures. This was a bit of escapism for me as I was a lonely kid and enjoyed reading about something I wanted to live like. I started my own stories but never finished them. Until now.

My father worked at General Dynamics on the river at this point in life where he designed interior decks for submarines. Sometime bringing his work home and worked all night. Him and Stinky would go out on the weekend and leave her niece 16 yrs. old or around that age with me to keep me company. She was pretty and we would listen to music, and she taught me how to play poker and dance, but my mind was on her boobs as always with me. A developing admirer of the boobs. Nothing went on between us but good times and good company. One day we visited her family in downtown, and they had an apartment and three kids. One girl named Nancy, her brother, and some little brat. Nancy's brother came to me and said Nancy wants to see you in the closet under the stairs. He and I went in, Nancy started to kiss me and then took her blanket off, and she was naked, and then grabbed my crotch. I didn't know what I was doing but she did. Nancy was 11 yrs. old like me. What worldly knowledge she had I thought. I was never brought back there again for some reason. Hmmm.

I walked to a three-story brick schoolhouse about a mile away and it was on the edge of the Thames River and there was a smaller old building on the river next to the school and it had a wood paddle wheel on the side that was used to run some belt driven machinery. This used to be an old gristmill, or something abandoned long ago.

This was the first time I was challenged by a school bully. He got me mad, and I pushed him down as the school bell rang to come in. How cool was that. An easy victory. One evening Dad and Stinker went out again, and I was left alone. Then my father came back by himself,

came to my cot, and sat on a chair. I could see that he was naked and trying to wake me up, but I acted as if I was sleeping, but he knew better because I started to shake and had my eyes closed. He talked to me in a strange way and finally said OK then and left. I never looked at him the same way again.

After that time, maybe a year and a half, things changed dramatically again. Myself and my younger brother David (I don't know where he was all that time) were sent to a foster home in Melrose Massachusetts, Gooch Street, with a foster family. The father, mother an older son and us. I think we were there about one year. The father was obsessed with collecting newspapers and the basement was head high with his collection. David and I were the slave labor to remove this stuff for days on end during the summer as we fought off the bugs and rats and put it all in a pickup truck many times over. We also had to strip the wallpaper in the bedrooms so they could re-paper them. Then mow the grass and pull the weeds in the flowerbeds. If that was not enough on school mornings when her son didn't finish his cereal before he went off to school, it was my job to finish the soggy mess before I left for school. I was in yet another 3-storey brick schoolhouse and in 6th grade currently. I excelled in art and sports there. I was asked to draw Hannibal crossing the Alps like in the book we read.

This was a school favorite story, and the teachers left my sketch on the chalkboard for several days so the whole school could come by and look. Then I was asked to tell the story about Hannibal to the younger kids. What a self-esteem booster that was, even though I hated public speaking (even today). For some reason, I also was the projector (reel-to-reel) operator any time there was something to be shown in the auditorium. I mean for all grades. I felt so important. I was 6 feet tall and the tallest person in the school. Teachers included. Then one day we had man come by to test us in track, broad jumping, and other sport related events. I ran the forty-yard dash and was off the world record by four tenths of a second, so he said. A major victory in that school. I won a presidential fitness badge and wore it all the time.

Every Sunday I went off to Catholic Church and then to bible classes after. Every Friday I had to go to confession and lie about

sinning. Forgive me father but I have sinned. I took a cookie from the forbidden cookie jar without permission. Say three Hail Mary's and two Our Fathers the priest would say. I made my Holy Communion and Confirmation while there. My father would come by every few weeks and take me bowling and to lunch. He bought me a Hamilton watch and things went a lot better with him and I after that.

I learned how to ice skate and played hockey in the winter on a frozen pond nearby, with my local friends. I was coerced into basketball because of my height but was too clumsy and couldn't dribble down my chin. They put me under the hoop so I could grab the ball and pass it off to someone that did not have retard problems. I also played center and pushed it off to another teammate that could dribble. Go figure. I started playing baseball in a little league team. Played the outfield and was a fair hitter. I liked this. Then I played on a Babe Ruth League, and all the kids would call me Jethro like on the Beverly Hillbillies as I was tall and clumsy. My uniform didn't fit right, and my batting slumped with the low self-esteem. I felt like a judge because I was on the bench a lot. However, I got through the season. One day while walking around I saw some trash being thrown out. There was a handle sticking out of a box, and I pulled it out. It was a beautiful sword. I had this flashback that I had held a sword like this before. I waved it around a few times fascinated by it and went and hid it under the front porch for use later in case of a medieval war or something. I don't know what I was thinking. I'm such a dreamer sometimes, even today.

The foster parents home in Melrose, Ma.

This town was hilly, and my friends and I made skateboards with plywood and roller skates. Then went down the sidewalks right past Anna Ross's house, my heart's desire. She had no interest in me. She always had an excuse that she was busy. She was getting some boobs on her. Oh well.

A kid in my school thought he was god's gift to sports and girls. I would go to his house and play hoops or catch. I needed the practice. He liked to pick on my little brother when I brought him along and I asked him to stop. He pushed David and made him cry. That was it. I punched him in the nose and made it bleed. The p---- went crying to his mother and she came out on the porch and said don't ever come back here again. He never said a word to me after that at school.

Then one day my father came to drive me off to who knows where again. I packed all my clothes (don't know what happened to my little

brother David, (this poor kid) and drove me to Calais, Maine. This was right across the river from St. Stephen, Canada. It was summer luckily, as the winters are brutal. Father was there working on a new power plant, and I was introduced to his new girlfriend. Her name was Robena. She eventually became my stepmom. One point of interest about her she had told me. She was in the Canadian Army at one time and was the secretary of the man that played Uncle Fester on the Adam's Family TV show. You know the one that screwed a light bulb into his mouth, and it lit up. He at one time was a Major. How weird that was from someone of his rank.

She had four children Karl, Michael, Kathy, and Jonathan all to be my new stepfamily. Kathy was my age (13) Karl was 4 yrs. older, Michael was 2 yrs. older, and Jonathan was 3 yrs. younger. When Michael got out of reform school, (he had issues) he would walk me across the bridge into Canada with our fishing poles, no big security checks for terrorist back then, they would just wave you through, and we would catch more trout than we could carry. Really, the first time I ever caught a fish. Karl was sharing a room with my dad and working with him on another power plant together. Soon after, Karl enlisted into the Navy. That is probably why he wanted to enlist. I mean sharing a room with my dad. My two future brothers and myself would throw darts at each other and they would stick in our heads and chest. Ouch. So funny. It's a miracle we still had two good eyes. How stupid that was. Ha Ha. Then one day me and my not yet stepsister was shipped off to Baptist youth camp in central Maine. That was fun, horseback riding, swimming, music lessons and of course church. I lived in a bunkhouse that held four of us. Some other kids had to sleep in a large army tent. I wanted to sleep in an army tent because it was cool man. I still have a picture of me and my friend from then. We did everything fun together. I once convinced a kid to pee on the barbed wire fence that was electrified to keep the horses in. Oops.

Me at Baptist youth camp in Maine. (On the left)

He had a shocking experience you might say.

Sometime shortly after the camp I was packed up again and brought to my grandmother's house (that my father built for her and George (Papa) her husband. This was the first time I had met this grandmother. This house was also in Thomaston, Ct. but way up a hill a few miles from downtown. This was on a dirt road and the only other house was across the street. We had 3 acres of fields and miles of forest behind. I was all alone for a while then my two young sisters were brought in sometime later, don't know where they were had been either. And they played all the time on the screened in back porch that ran the length of the house. This house was a single story and was on an incline so the house had a basement and sliding doors that would step out to the backyard. It looked like a trailer home with a basement. I slept in a bedroom in the basement alone and it was kind of creepy going down there in the

night. No one from the area to play with except my dog Taffy. (I don't remember what became of Woody.) She was a cocker spaniel and loved to roam the woods with me. Hunting with my bow and fishing along the pond, she was always by my side. I became very proficient with a bow and got into an archery class at school. (A showoff my instructor would say.) When my father came by, we would do things like rifle shoot at targets he set up in a field. I was exceptionally good at this, and it irritated him because I was a better shot. He did not want to get beat again and that stopped. I was just starting junior high and caught a bus that I had to walk to where the local kids waited but they were older, and we didn't mingle together after school.

I once bagged a pheasant in flight with a special barbed arrow designed for bird hunting that I saw at the local K Mart that Papa George bought for me. I brought the bird to my grandmother for skinning. She gave it to my Papa George, and nothing ever became of it. He was never a hunter, I guess. George was on a bowling team although and would take me with him as company as I was bored most of the time. I remember watching the Wizard of Oz for the first time at the bowling alley. I was fascinated by this fairy land and wanted to live there. Even today. On Sundays, he loved to watch the girl's roller derby on TV and curse. I learned some new words from him, and Nana would get mad when I repeated them. I also was bored enough to try football by myself, but only place kicking. I would set the ball on the tee and try to launch it over the tree line that separated our two fields. Then bring the tee and kick it back. Got pretty dam good at it also. Lots of practice alone.

One day this girl from school came down my road on a horse and asked if I wanted to go for a ride with her. I was so intimidated by her command of this horse and I in a strange trembling voice said to her, "*I have to go in the house to help my grandmother*".

She never came back. What a ladies' man. I was there for about two years. This kind of life kept me out of trouble, set me straight, and taught me about nature and all things wild, like the 6-foot black snake that slid over my shoes in the woods as I watched in horror and Taffy

21

barked. It seemed like a mile long as slow as it slithered. Come to find out it was harmless, but my eyes told me do not move Bobby.

Sometimes my Uncle George and Aunt Ann with George Jr. and little Stevie would visit. He was my father's older brother and Nana would always say how he was the good son and make his favorite dinner. Boston baked beans in the pressure cooker. Oh, how she fussed over that. Then I would take George and little Stevie out into the woods with the intent to scare them. They were city kids, but the snake never showed, to my disappointment. Taffy and I were upset.

Nana was diabetic and I saw her many times shoot the insulin in her legs. I attribute my diabetes from her as it skips a generation. Diabetes isn't anything to ignore as it has many bad medical issues that comes with it. A long-life span is not one of them. Nana was always busy knitting slippers for everyone most of her free time. Personally, I loved them and wish she could be here to make more.

Then one summer day my father took me away again, this time to Cape Cod in Mass. He had an apartment on the Cape Cod Canal, which separated the Cape from the mainland with two large span bridges over the canal that you had to use to get on the peninsula. He was working on another power plant nearby and bought me a beautiful salt-water rod and real. I practiced my technique of casting in the canal several times and was ready for the big ones. So, one morning 6:30 am, he brought me to a rocky peninsular within eyesight of the plant. This was made up of many large rocks that jutted out at the end of the canal. I cast off for the first time then slipped on the slimy part of a rock, fell on and broke my rod in half. It seemed like forever until he came to get me at the end of the day. He never bought me another one to try again.

Dad liked me to sleep in the same bed with him and one night I awoke with him fondling me and he said it was ok. I went and slept on the couch and stayed there always. Then one day my brother David showed up and stayed until we moved. David slept with him, the poor kid was too young to know how perverted he was, and he never said a word about anything going on. Maybe he thought this was normal behavior.

Chapter 3

A New Family

One day in the summer we moved into a house and here comes the new wife Robena and family, Michael, Kathy, Jonathan. Then later my two sisters Twinkie and Pruny. Aka, Loretta, and Lorraine also David. We all lived there for a short time until it became too much for my stepmother and father to support. My sisters and brother were shipped out to foster family's separately never to be seen for many years later until they were adults and found me years later with the dawn of the internet.

Onset, Ma.

23

My stepmother's children all stayed of course. Me and Michael had a bedroom together upstairs Jonathan and David then Kathy her own. Mom and Dad downstairs. This was a two-story wood frame home with a big front porch and one block from Onset Beach. A beautiful tourist destination. The house also had a history. Mrs. Peck a backyard neighbor said to me over the fence one day. Don't you know this house is haunted! There was a man that lived there alone, and he shot himself in the head in the upstairs bedroom. I mentioned it to the family, and they just didn't pay no mind about it. However, it wasn't too long before mother started noticing things like the stove being turned down if something was boiling. Or our winter shoes that were supposed to be in the mudroom moved there if we left them in the kitchen, and the door shut tight to the basement if we left it ajar. Then one night my sister woke up and went screaming from her room because the chair was rocking. Yikes.

My brother Mike and I would make model cars and airplanes at a table in the basement, and I would feel the ghost's presence over my shoulder. Mike didn't. Then sometimes our models and supplies on the table would be artfully arranged by him and my brother would get upset and tell me not to touch his stuff again or he would kick my ass. When I was alone in the basement, I would talk to this ghost to try to get a reply of some sort, but he was not spontaneous like that. He seemed friendly and helpful, and I wasn't afraid. I guess he sensed that. (Red rum-red rum, he he.) So, me and my stepmother, the only ones that new it was there just going on with our lives and let it be. Well one night I woke up and heard footsteps across the linoleum floor heading down the hall and toward the stairs. I saw the translucent image pass by the open bedroom door. He started down the stairs, creek, creek, and I got out of bed and watched this ghostly apparition descend and I followed it down the enclosed staircase and then it turned left and proceeded across the dining room as I watched from the bottom of the steps. Then he turned the corner into the kitchen as I watched it dissipate. I was the only one that witnessed this. I was mesmerized. Still a big event I want to see again. I felt I had a reach into another world.

Anyway, life went on in Onset, I was in high school 9th grade, my father was always on my ass about something, stand up straight, pull your shoulders back or I'll make you wear a back brace. Apparently, he thought I was a wimpy kid until I shoveled snow out of the driveway at 5 am many mornings so he could go to work. Michael was a senior, and he taught me how to siphon gas so we could get to school in his Opal station wagon that mother gave him. One night we went out our upstairs.

(Note to self) My dad and stepmom always treated me as a troublesome kid. I was at one time in life.

bedroom window and down the porch trellis then pushed his Opal station wagon down the street until we were out of earshot of the engine starting. Siphoned some gas, mostly in my mouth as this was my first time, we pushed the car back into the driveway and climbed back up the trellis and got in bed. Then dad came up and asked where we had been. Oh, nowhere we said as we reeked of gas fumes. Then he pulled out his Zippo lighter, lit it up, came closer, and spoke. Let's start over. Were where you? We didn't do that again. Not at night anyway. At this location Dad had purchased a Ford station wagon with the fake wood siding running from hood to tailgate. He loved this car and installed upgraded speakers and a tape deck. Everywhere we went was a Herb Alpert and The Tijuana Brass experience. I liked it also but not my sister. I still like it to this day.

Onset was the best place a teenage boy could live in the summer months. Lots of young girls came with their families just to see me, so I liked to think. There was Linda O, who had a cool Mustang and Genevieve G, both from Danbury Ct. But didn't' know each other. However, Linda was brought up a good Catholic girl and had to be in at sunset. Gen and I had to walk everywhere, and she could stay out late. And we would kiss behind the big rock on the beach. That was so romantic i thought.

There lots of fun things to do in the summer months. I had my buddy Timothy S and Gene C that I would hang with and who were volunteer firefighters. I was the new guy in the department and basically rode

along, watched, and rolled up hoses. In the summer when the siren went off, we would run to the station to jump on the back of the fire truck. It was only a few blocks from the beach. The girls were impressed as we hung on the fire truck whisking by them.

Then one day along came Marilyn H from Taunton, Ma. A tall girl of Portuguese parents whose mother worked at the pier taffy house. Burgers and shakes as well as hand pulled salt-water taffy. Only open in the summer of course. Yummy stuff. Her dad had a boat in the bay that I never saw move. They had a trailer home over the bluff in a trailer park for the summer months. I would sneak over, and Marilyn would look out the front window to see if anyone was coming and pull down her pants and let me have at it. What I wonderful girl that I fell in love with and carried on for a few years when we could see each other. My father caught on and said that better be puppy love mister.

Living in Onset was a great experience for a former city kid as I would go to the beach around the corner in the cooler months with my clam rake, clam ring, and dig up a 5-gallon pail of them in short order. If they fit through the ring, I had to throw it back. Simple enough as there were plenty and my mother would steam or boil them and with a side dish like corn on the cob. Striped bass where so plentiful that when we swam out to the floating platform in summer and dive off in the deeper water, they would swim by and rub against you. We could fish for them and catch more than needed at any time. Lobster as well if you were taught how to grab them barehanded. The learning curve was a bitch though.

A couple of seasons went by and again, we moved. This time to Raynham, Ma. We lived on Nicholas St. Dad, mom, Kathy, Jonathan, and me. We were in a fancy new subdivision and that was high class living back then. We all would sit around the tube at night and watch the original Star Trek with William Shatner as Capt. Kirk and Leonard Nimoy as Spock. This was dad's favorite show. He liked a little fantasy, I guess. One day when my mother was doing laundry, she found a pack of cigarettes under my clothes in my dresser. She showed dad and he came in the bedroom one morning and pulled them out. Oh f---. He stuck one in my mouth and lit it. Smoke it he said. I

did a little and he said OK then. You know how to smoke. I just didn't want you looking like some A-- hole trying to smoke. However, don't do this around here.

I went to finish 9th grade at Bridgewater Raynham High School. This is where I met my best friend to this day, Ken H. I met him as we were both trying out for the baseball team in the outfield. I was running backwards to catch the ball with the sun in my eyes and tripped, fell on my back and he caught it over my body. He said I never met anyone so clumsy in my life. Been best friends ever since. He still says shit like that to me and everyone else.

I took French class there and for the first time I learned the correct pronunciation of my last name from my French teacher. Go figure. Not 4jet but 4shey. Or something like that. I don't know how to spell that and make it sound right. Anyway, I was too skinny for football even though the football coach who also was my math teacher wanted me as a receiver because of my speed in track, but I was afraid of being hit and breaking in half, I guess. He brought me out of class one time into the corridor, poked his finger in my chest, and said for me to show up at practice. I never did. I stayed with track and field instead. I was very quick runner and tried pole-vaulting, once. I did well in sports because there were not many black kids that went to that school. Don't get me wrong, I am not prejudiced at all. They just run faster. I was never one to be too judgmental or prejudice being how I grew up with many people of many ethnicity's.

Taunton wasn't far and I would hitchhike to Marilyn's house, sit on the couch for hours, and watch TV, with her mother looming and hovering around every corner. Couldn't even catch a smooch. Sometimes we would go out in the woods behind her house and smooch. One day I was hitching a ride from her house and this guy in a Corvette (a French word like Chevrolet) stopped to pick me up. He put a dollar bill on the dash and said when I take off try to reach for it and it's yours. I was thrust back in the seat and couldn't do it. Never forgot that.

Well before you know it, we moved again another year later. This was getting old. This time it was Alpha, N.J. near Phillipsburg N.J. When summer came, I arranged for me to go back to Onset and work at Carbo's sub shop again and stayed at a rooming house for the summer months with the old woman that owned it. Rose T. She was 85 and would always tell me to shave off those sideboards as I started to develop some Elvis sideburns. It was the beginning of summer, and the house was full of college guys that ran the ice cream trucks all over the Cape. Rowdy bunch as you can imagine. My friend Linda from Danbury, and her parents lived right across the street in the summer months. But like I mentioned she was a good catholic girl and respectful so no hanky panky going on with her. At 16, I was full of hanky panky. Life was good in the summer there and I went around barefoot from the beach down the two blocks of Main Street with all the little shops and open-air restaurants. Not to forget the outdoor amphitheater for summer concerts on the hillside overlooking the beach. A kid I went to high school with had started a band and would play there. They were exceptionally good at copying some of the bands of that era and went on to play some bigger gigs. Some of my friends would drive me to work at the sub shop and I made them free sandwiches. Then come and pick me up at 9:00 when I closed. I was back on the fire department with my pals and life was good again totally on my own. So now, I'm hanging with three girls, and they don't know about each other. Linda was not allowed out after dark, and Marilyn could until eight. Gen, well Gen all night. We would go out to the big rock at the end of the beach and make out behind it. Hanky panky, yeah.

At the end of summer, I didn't want to go to New Jersey where my family was and decided to stay on the Cape. School started in September and my boss Carl W (Carbo's sub shop) became my mentor and was my acting legal guardian for that time. My father called him, and he signed the papers assuming guardianship. Carl taught me how to drive a 3 speed on the column shift with the company Ford van. Then I would drive out of town to pick up the fresh bread at a bakery each morning in the summer months or on the weekends because of school, with him watching me drive as I was still on a permit license.

Soon after I bought a 57 Chevy two door for 250 bucks. This had a 283 cubic inch with a three speed Hurst shift on the floor. A real chick magnate. The only problem was I didn't have a full license yet, so I had my friends drive me around in it because there where issues letting me drive certain hours with only a permit. My buddy Doug B. at work who was in the Air Force locally had his wife take me for the driving test. He was like a big brother to me. Doug was also on the fire dept. diving squad. I once watched him bring up a man that went swimming in a small pond and got hung up on something under water. That was the first time I witnessed a dead body. It was like a water balloon. Poor guy was home on leave from the Army.

Anyway, I started 10th grade at Wareham H.S. and took the bus back and forth. I went to work at the sub shop after school and sometimes had to walk the 3 miles or hitchhike to and from or after work at 9 pm. Fall and winter came along with the snow, ice, and wind as you might image being on the bay near the ocean. It was a real bitch when I couldn't get a ride as the town people stayed in on those cold days and nights. So, I walked the whole distance freezing and on the street with cars flying by within inches of death. There were no sidewalks outside of Onset. I had heard about the pervert that was living nearby with his big black Cadillac cruising for boys. One day he passed me and turned around to pick me up, but I didn't care as I was freezing. I jumped in and told him where I was going (to work), and he seemed odd and didn't say anything then he started rubbing his crotch and I think he pulled it out. I looked out the side window until he dropped me off. Wow, I will never do that again I said to myself. F------ pervert.

My teachers at school learned about me working after school and living alone and passed it on to the superintendent of schools for that district. I was deferred from doing homework as I had to work to survive and was a living testament of self-reliance as a student could be. Always clean, nails trimmed, dressed nice, clean cut etc. When officials came to the school, I was called to the principal's office for a looky loo. Just to show them how a self-reliant kid of 16 yrs. could be like. I was a model student according to the principal, and a great role model. After that experience, I have always kept myself that way even now. Well except for my hippy days (Coming up later). My grades

were always straight C's because I didn't have to do homework. That was the deal. The town was dead in the winter months. About 5,000 people. Then 50,000 in the summer. Nothing to do in the winter. Not even a movie theater. During the fall months, one year I got a job with a man named Marshall Bugg. He was from Tennessee and moved to the Cape as he had a relative there or something. He taught me how to drive a 10-speed moving truck. An old double clutch behemoth. You had to step on the clutch, put it neutral, step on the clutch again, and then shift. We loaded and delivered housefuls of furniture, and cranberries. The Ocean Spray cranberry factory was in Onset of all places. There where cranberry bogs all over the local areas. Mostly in remote areas. In the winter, we would skate on them. In the summer, go skinny-dipping in them. Some of the summer girls would come there just to giggle and point at us. So amused, I guess. Sizing us up, I think. Then in the fall the bog workers with a vibrating machine would shake the cranberry bushes to make the berries float to the top. They would put them in wood crates, and I would load them up and drive to the factory. All you could eat by the way at the bogs. Still love them today.

Then I found out about a bay house from some friends from school were a girl decided to stay on and live there year-round when her parents left after summer. She was a little older and would hold big parties on the weekend in her three-story house on the water. Soon many kids from school would show up. Lots of light skinned blacks who were known as Cape Verdeans' whose ancestors were from an island off Africa they said. I just get along with everyone anyway. There was this one blonde headed girl from school that everybody wanted, and she would show up sometimes and hang with my history teacher Mr. G. He would only show when she was there. Lots of booze and music. This was the Motown era and that's what was mostly played at that house. We would dance, drink, and have a good time. This was my introduction to alcohol.

As the school year was coming to an end my father called me at the rooming house and asked about my grades. I wasn't sure about passing even though I got straight C's. He said himself and your brother Karl are coming to get you tomorrow so be ready. At this point

in my life, I had gone to 9 different schools in 3 states. That is an obscurity right there. They came and drove me to the house they were living at in Alpha, New Jersey. A red brick single story with a full built out basement. Kitchen, laundry, pool table, bedroom, fireplace and more. I slept down there. It was like my own apartment. There was a large field next to the house and we would play baseball there until someone complained because I would hit the ball past the end of the field and hit a passing car sometimes. My sister always whined about me pitching too hard for her to hit the ball. Such a wussy. One time my brother Mike stayed for a few weeks and was into smoking weed. One night he said let's go into the bathroom and I will show you how to do this. We did and I got a buzz then we went into the bedroom we shared and giggled for a while as he danced on the bed naked. Weirdo. Our mother asked what the smell was downstairs, and Mike showed her the pot. She took it from him and said I need to show my friends so they know what it looks like because they thought their kids might be smoking it. She even took some puffs on it and chocked.

I started school in Phillipsburg N.J. for a while and I hated it there and wanted to quit. I got a job at a place called Nytronics, which made transistor parts for military rockets. Repetitious though. Not a bad job and met a cute girl there and had a few dates with her since she had a car. I met her Polish family and they seemed nice. Well, that didn't last long as my father said you are going to join the Navy. They will make a man out of you. He drove me to the recruiting office and signed me up as you had to have a parent sign if you are less than 18 yrs. old. This was done at the Navy recruiter office across the river in Easton, Pa. in 1969. Putting me in the Navy was his answer to his issues with me.

Chapter 4
Anchors Away

I was shipped by bus from the recruiting office one day to the Navy shipyard in Philadelphia, sworn in with many others, and made some friends right off. After that, we were brought to a train station and put on sleeper cars for the long trip to Chicago. Once there we were put on a bus to Great Lakes Naval Training Facility just north of Chicago. Upon arrival, there was our company commander waiting for us and we piled out like a bunch of misfits that we collectively were. It didn't take long before we had to get in single file, try to march to the chow hall, as it was dinner time, and talk about standing out in a crowd with our street clothes on, we did. Luckily, no one was allowed to look or talk to us as we went through the line and then ate. They were recruits as well. Then off to our temporary barracks for the night. I don't know how I was picked to stand guard with a rifle over the water fountain so no one could use it. Shoot to kill anyone trying to drink water from the fountain. It wasn't loaded. That would be an accident waiting to happen. I was still in the clothes I came with and stood there all night until breakfast at 5:00 am. How weird this was. Then to the clothing building for our bell-bottom pants and denim shirt, our daily outfits. Oh, and the hat of course. Then to the barber for a military haircut and shave so we all looked alike. We were then marched to our permanent barracks and Chief Cutchin had each of us stand at attention and turn around toe to heel and snap your heals back at attention.

Me and Jerome who I met at inauguration where the two runners up. He beat me at the fancy footwork and became the RPOC that is the recruit petty officer in charge. The top dog. I don't know how I was even considered. Good footwork I guess and tall. He led the company brandishing a sword at the head of the company as we

marched everywhere. I wanted that position badly. I don't know why as I was always very shy and not outspoken at all. More of a follower than leader. Just wanted to be somebody of importance for once I think. Boot camp was actually a breeze for me. I'm not sure how but I won our company (464) an athletic flag to march with because I was the fastest rope climber in the whole division. I became Captain of the rope climbing squad. I didn't think I went up faster, but I sure slid down faster. OH, we were all glad to be there in the summer months, winter is a bitch. I was assigned to an upper rack and my buddy Dale got the bottom. I was taller than him and could get up there easier. He was the one that carried the flag with company 464 at the front of the company.

We went through many obstacle courses, parade marching, 21 count rifle handling, shoulder to hands then tap the ground and back again. I loved it. One night I was put on regimental fence patrol with someone from another company. With rifle and special arm band we patrolled our section of the fence and caught a recruit trying to go over the fence. He saw us and took off into the three-story barracks nearby and we ran after him through other company quarters and finally found him crying under someone's bunk. We brought him to regimental headquarters on the base. The poor guy wanted to go home. There were lots of them like that.

One day we all had to get more shots of medicine and stand in formation with our pants and underwear down to our ankles as the doctor administered the feared bycilyn shot into the ass cheek. This was a needle as big as a dart and hurt. The guy next to me passed out onto the floor as the doctor approached him. Thanks buddy, I was next.

I learned how to break down and put back a 45-caliber pistol blindfolded. Went to the rifle range and got 20 bulls' eye's out of 21 shots with the M1 A sharpshooter the chief told me. We were all glad to be there in the summer months, winter is a bitch. I was assigned to an upper rack and my buddy Dale got the bottom. I was taller than him and could get up there easier. He was the one that carried the flag with company 464 at the front of the company.

33

Typical day at boot camp

At one point, we all had what was called service week where we were assigned a job around the boot camp for that week. I got lucky due to my marksmanship and winning an athletic flag and went to the armory building and cleaned rifles all day. This was a very sought-after detail. We didn't have to show up until eight and left at four. We could drink soda and listen to music all day. The other men went to the chow hall at 4 am to peel potatoes, chop veggies and didn't get back until 7 pm after they cleaned the kitchen. By the way, they put something in the food so that no one could get an erection. Salt peter. Clever idea. Who wants to walk around with a hard on in boot camp anyway? The gay types kept their desire's a close secret to themselves.

What a time I had in boot camp. One funny part of this was someone came up with the idea of fly races. We would catch some flies, put them in a refrigerator (The chief's fridge, he didn't know) and this would put them in a semi coma state. Then take them out and tie a piece of thread on one leg and cup them in your hand. This warmed them up and they were ready to race. Then two of us would each hold one and let them go. Buzz, buzz and up and down they flew because of

34

the thread. Whichever one stayed in flight the longest won. Of course, we exchanged some cash to whomever picked the winner. What meat head thought this up? I liked it.

Well after 9 weeks it was time to graduate, and the chief gave us some documents to read and pick what you would want to do as an occupation. We had five choices and I picked four in aviation but first picked the Seabee's you know the construction part of the military. I was told that I had to pick another occupation as all Seabee's went to Vietnam and I was only 17 and had to be 18. Therefore, I picked submarines an all-volunteer occupation. Little did I know what was ahead. After a week back in Jersey on leave at my parent's place, I was shipped off (a navy slang word) to Groton Connecticut at the sub-base across the Thames River from where I use to live. Go figure. I was put in a barracks with men from all ranks that wanted to be in the sub service. It went well there and one day as we were all in formation for roll call. A Chief P.O. was looking for a volunteer to go to Cape Cod with him in a Navy truck to pick up some beds at Otis Air Force base near where I worked at the sub sandwich shop. This was about a 4-hour drive. I raised my hand in a split second and told him I was from there. Well, we left the base in a flatbed truck and as soon as he could, he pulled over to a liquor store and got a bottle of scotch. Driving along he would tip it up and then said would you like some son. I took some swigs from it even though I had never tried this before and got shit faced. When we arrived, I was so drunk he had to load the beds himself. I was passed out on the seat. I don't remember the drive back and have never touched the stuff since.

I went through some unusual training there such as the 100-foot vertical water filled tower, which was to simulate an escape from a sub with closed hatches that you went through and then closed again. This was called SETT. Submarine Escape Training Tower. Then in a separate building, the diving bell that put 50 lbs. per sq. inch of pressure on you. Normally its 14.7 lbs. in everyday life. When you go down then up you start freezing and then sweating. Maybe it was the other way around? This guy next to me didn't use proper technique blowing his ears out to relive the pressure and his inner ear or fluid blew out. On me of course. Yuk

Submarine Escape Training Tower (SETT)

The base had the first nuke sub (Nautilus) docked there for repairs or something and I would sometimes board the vessel and have lunch with the few onboard. The Navy sub service is known for the best food in all the military. Just like mom cooked it. The base cafeteria wasn't bad either. Everywhere I went I spent a lot of time saluting as there where many officers on base. I should have duct taped my hand up on my forehead in a permanent salute. I went to classes most of the day and sometimes evening with a break between. I also got my GED while there with no problems. My aptitude test showed that I was a good problem solver and had mechanical skills and good with my hands. I kept getting pushed into an engine room position, but I never liked getting greasy. I went on some training missions on some old diesel-powered subs and ended up in the bowels cleaning grease and everything the beast would expel under the deck plates. This was not for me, and I wanted out. I non volunteered myself out as this was an all-volunteer position and got yelled at in a room of officers at a hearing. They then sent me to a different barracks with like men. I did get a chance to work with the Seabee's building the local VFW hall off base as I awaited reassignment. This is what I enjoyed, outside in the elements working at building something that would be there forever. Not cooped up in the bowels of a hot submarine doing the same thing repeatedly. To this day, I still cannot do that for long.

My new assignment came along, and I was shipped to Norfolk, VA the largest naval base in the world. I was assigned to the USS Springfield CLG 7 the flagship of the 6th fleet. Guided Missile Cruiser Light. The Admiral would travel on this ship and even the deck plates down below had to be buffed and shiny, as I know well. My main job was maintenance of the forward engine room such as fixing or replacing old valves that where packed with asbestos insulation and wrapped in canvas. I pulled this stuff out with my hands and no respirator. I could have been subjected to mesothelioma. They were not aware of this disease then I guess, and many veterans suffer with this today and die too soon. I also changed the oil in the spring bearings that supported the propeller shafts and take gauge readings. I would crawl and bend into all the nooks and crannies of this ship to read a gauge.

We had to leave base one day and cruise down the Atlantic heading South as there was a hurricane heading up the coast and all ships must head out to sea and through it or else get banged up at the dock. We went head on into the swells that had to be 40-50-foot-tall, and all four props would come out of the water when we crested on the top, the ship would shake like a tin can. Myself and two buddies snuck out on deck and tied ourselves to the bulkhead to watch as the ship went down between the swells, and it looked as if they would fold over on us then we popped up. This was strictly forbidden, and I don't remember how we did it. Stupid kid stuff. Then down to the Virgin Islands etc. on the way to Guantanamo Bay Cuba. It got ridiculously hot and humid below decks. I was working hard carrying 5-gallon buckets of used spring bearing oil up and down the ladders (stairs) and I bent to get a cold drink from the fountain and when I stood up, I collapsed, and an officer behind me grabbed my limp body. I was dragged to a bench and given water that spilled everywhere, as I was shaking so bad. Then dragged to sickbay and given fluids by the ships doc. He told me to go up on deck and relax the rest of my duty and as I headed that way my chief who saw me in the corridor told me to get back in the engine room. So, I did. Never did get along with him. What an asshole.

Cuba was incredibly beautiful and had great beaches. Once and a while we got to go to a secluded beach for military personnel, and drink and swim or relax. The inlet we swam in was blocked off from the sea because of all the sharks there. A friend and I scaled the rock face wall to the top and saw these monitor lizards about six feet long and standing about two feet at the head. Holy shit, this was too much for a Yankee boy to deal with, so we climbed down fast. The next thing we did was to walk along the beach and discovered a newly hatched nest of Ridley Sea turtles wiggling towards the water. We scooped them up in our sailor's cap's and gently delivered them at the water's edge. It took a few hat full's. As we walked along the beach, we came across a chain link fence that was pushed over and walked past disregarding the sign that said entering Cuban territory, or something like that. Actually, it was old, rusted, and hard to read. Not long after we heard someone on a bullhorn in Spanish say something but couldn't make

out from where, so we continued. There was machine gun fire from the cliff over our heads into the surf. Got the point and ran back over the fence. WOW.

One night some of us went to the Copacabana club for drinks and watch the pretty girls dancing on stage. Clothes on dam it. Well, we started drinking 151 proof rum, which I never had before, as well as some of the other boys either. We had a curfew, and the cattle trailer came to bring us back to ship, yes that's how they moved us about, like cows. Our ship and other ships personnel climbed in, and we started a war, go figure right. Fists went flying, chock holds and blood. When the truck slowed down for the stop sign, we used big, Dale K (a big Swede) as a battering ram and broke open the ramp and we all piled out in the street with fists flying. I avoided as much as possible because of my thin self-did not have the street fighting knowledge some did but I learned fast and dodged as many fists as I could, came through with some bruises. When we were delivered at our ship, two of my buddies had to drag me up the gangplank, as I was shit faced, they took my hand, and saluted the boarding officer and he said get him below decks now.

The crew quarters where extremely hot somewhere around 100 + degrees all the time. You would wake up in a pool of sweat in a canvas rack every morning. Then hop in the shower for a Navy shower which was turn on water, turn off water, lather, and turn the water back on to rinse. OH, and do not bend over to pick up the soap. Ha Ha. We finally left there after many training exercises with the missiles and 6" guns and sometimes the Marines on board would drop hand grenades overboard to simulate torpedo attacks, then the call for battle stations was broadcast. So back to Norfolk we sailed. Never did like being below deck I'm much more into the sightseeing cruise on deck. Love Boat style.

Chapter 5
A Stupid Mistake

Once back in Norfolk we were all given a three-day pass. I decided to catch a bus and head up to Cape Cod for a visit. Saw my friends, decided to stay a little longer aka (awhol), went to Hyannis Port, and got a room at a rooming house. Then I got a job at the Howard Johnson's on Main St, what was I thinking. I told the manager I was just discharged and got hired on right away washing dishes. Things went well for a week until the man that rented the rooms came to me one night and said son, are you awhol? The FBI was here looking for you.

I said yes sir.

He told them I was not there. He then went and got some coffee and cookies and we talked. He said that he was in the Army and went awhol twice. Then he suggested that I go to the Navy recruiting office in town and turn myself in. So, I shaved the mustache and Elvis's sideburns put on my uniform and walked there. When I told the chief, I was awhol he freaked and said I don't know what to do with awhol. He said I must make some calls then gave me the keys to the Navy car and some cash and said go to the store down the street pick up some sandwiches and a playboy magazine while I'm figuring this out. I did, and we sat for hours eating and admiring the girls in the magazine while waiting on the shore patrol to get me. Well, these two yahoos from the south somewhere didn't know how they got to Hyannis Port or how to get back. So here I am sitting in the back of the van in a cage handcuffed, directing them to a base in Newport Rhode Island. It was at night, and we stopped at a McDonalds, as we were all hungry. I order a big Mac meal at the counter in handcuffs and thought how strange that had to look. Got checked in at the base and given a bed, not in a cell. The next morning, I was given bus ticket and sent to Times

Square in NYC to catch a bus back to the base. I had to check into a room they provided if you call it that. A 6' by 10' room with a bed and no more. The next morning, I walked to the New York Port Authority terminal that had busses, trains etc. a large place. I had papers saying I was under arrest and not allowed to talk to anyone about it or drink alcohol etc.

So, I walk into this bar and order a beer. I turn around and there sits my boot camp buddy Dusty with someone. I holler out, Dusty, long time no see as I walk over there. He was giving me some odd look, I sat next to him, and the other man not dressed like military across from us. Sandy was kicking my shin, which was odd, then he said let me out as he pushed me and took off running thru the port authority with this man pursuing him and me pursuing both. Three stooges' stuff. Well, the man was out of shape and stopped, then I stopped and asked what was going on. Dusty was under arrest he said, and he was escorting him in. I fell for this and said I was also. He then told me that he would escort me to Norfolk on the bus. I am an 18-yr. old kid and believed anything. I still do. Stupid adult stuff. Most of us react to fear and not the facts. I feared what was next.

On the way there, I sat next to the window with him next to me. It was late, the bus was full of sailors, and we tried to keep warm with our p-coats on backwards up around our necks. A couple of hours later the man's hand went on my knee. I looked and put it back on his lap. A simple mistake, right. Shortly after his hand landed near my crotch and that was not a mistake. I peeled back my p-coat and elbowed him in the solar plexus 3 times, and he was gasping for air. I yelled out this mother f......is a homo. He changed seats and got off at the next stop. After a couple of days at F barracks while waiting for new orders, he called there for me, and they got me on the phone with him. He said I am sorry, and I live in Norfolk, and he wanted me to come over. I said OK, can I bring a couple of friends along. Click. Never heard from the s.o.b again. While at F barracks, which was a building of total misfits except for the part I was in with the shore patrol on the first floor. I was given the job of patrolling a certain part of the building that had an entry with bars and a lock. They gave me a billy club and I had to walk the floor to keep an eye on activity and report. I don't know how

I got this assignment. This unit was full of drug addicts and queers. One homo grabbed the club and said my that's a big one. Do not touch that fag, I said. Then one night I went with the shore patrol to break up a fight at the enlisted men's club on the base. I don't know why they picked my skinny little ass for this stuff. Well, I had the billy club you know, and I would use it in a conflict. Once there, low and behold who is in the middle of this ruckus and being uncooperative? Big Dale K (the swede) from my ship, drunk and throwing around tables and chairs at everyone. The guys I went with couldn't control him. I spoke up and said let me try, he is my shipmate. Dale saw me and started to loosen up, and we talked. He said that he would go peacefully if I handcuffed him and brought him to the brig with the other shore patrol men. Never saw him again.

Once returned to the ship I was given 30 days restriction and extra duty as well. The captain was easy on me because he was in the submarine service and non-volunteered out as well. So, life in the Navy went on and out at sea my Chief said as part of your discipline you will stay on watch below decks and do your job for 72 hours straight, no break. I tried but on the third morning, I was caught standing up and holding my clipboard with the gauge readings that I took and was falling asleep. My chief started in on me and I had enough. I punched him with a hook and knocked him over into some pipes or something like that. That started a big deal, and I was sent to the ship's doc, and I asked to see a physiatrist at the base. I wanted out at this point, as I was acting irrational a lot. The shrink listened to me and concluded that I had claustrophobia. He was right because I didn't act like this unless I was below decks in tight spaces. I asked for a transfer to the Seabee's since I was 18 and the answer came back that I was being given an Honorable Discharge for medical reasons. So, there I went back to F barracks in Norfolk VA. With a different set of misfits in a different section. The person next to my rack was getting out because he wet his bed every night. He did this on purpose just to get discharged as a misfit. Others would claim they missed their mommy's and cried at night. I was glad to get out of there.

Chapter 6
Another life change

Once out of the Navy I went back to Onset to be with my friends and then worked back at Carbo's sub shop where I was employed at the age of 14 until the Navy. Luckily making sub sandwiches didn't bring on claustrophobia. I started work at that age because my father would put a bowl on my head and give me a haircut. I looked like MO on the three stooges. He said if you don't like it get a job and pay for it. I did. After the Navy, the sub shop had to hire me back as a veteran because it was mandatory of previous employers nationwide. I worked there for a while until one day I was walking past a construction site next door and this man named Victor B. (Italians did most of the construction work back then where I was from) he asked if I wanted to make extra money digging a hole. Sure, I said. I was a dam good hole digger and he put me on full time. He did many jobs in and around Boston, re-pointing the brickwork on old buildings. Meaning scrape the mortar out of the joints between the bricks and apply new mortar. Sometimes tar and gravel roofs. I had to buy new shoelaces often because they would be covered with hot tar and had to be cut off each night. I wasn't smart enough to cover them with something, stupid adult stuff again. Victor was the worst driver I had ever been around; he would stomp on the gas then let off repeatedly. I said Victor, let me drive. He got the point, I guess I'm not the first one to say that to him. So, for now on I did all the driving even though my license had expired while in the Navy. Even when we had other men in the truck qualified to drive. One day we were working on the side of a six-story old brick apt. building, up on a hand crank scaffold to start at the top on down. The crank was stuck one day, and I hollered at Victor down below that we could not get down. Up the stairs he went and stuck his head out of someone's apartment window to reach the handle. He couldn't get it

to work, I said here's the problem and released a lever, and the handle started spinning right into his head. He got mad and ripped off his daily uniform (white dress shirt) and threw it to the ground and left. He had ripped the shirt off on many occasions by the way. One day he came to the job site all excited and said for us to all get in, you will not believe what I saw. We drove to the Boston Common and there was a group of Hare Krishna's all-in robe's and singing and chanting as Victor drove around the block a few times to give them the finger. Crazy ass Italian.

Many times, we had to stop on the way home so he could go visit some of his friends in the back room of a pizza restaurant and play poker for an hour or so. Wink wink! Come to find out Victor was part of the infamous Costa Nostra (AKA) our thing as some translates this. Sicilian part of Italy. In other words, the Mafia. We did a job across the street from the Bunker Hill Monument one time and were told not to look at the blonde-haired person that comes in and out of the building we were working on. As she was the girlfriend of the #1 hit man in Boston. Therefore, we tried not to, but she would wave at us and smile. Trouble making bitch. Victor would invite me to his home for dinner to be friendly with his hairy, ugly daughter he wanted me to marry, YUK. Then one day on the way to work he asked me if I remembered this bank we drove past about every day in Dorchester, and I said yes, and he started to tell me how him and a buddy wanted to pull a bank robbery and I was supposed to drive the getaway car. And with the daughter thing looming, I had to move away so Victor couldn't find me, I moved in with my friend Timmy.

Timmy was a town cop now and I stayed with him in a small house. Sometimes in the summer he would pull over some kids from out of town and if the car smelled like weed, he would confiscate it and tell them don't let me catch you with this again. We usually had all the free weed we could smoke. When the tourist left, we moved into a small home on the bay in Onset, very cozy. Then one day my friend Ray F from Onset came by with his girlfriend and her friend Sherrie. She liked me right off and she hardly ever got away from her parents' house in Brockton. We did it before the afternoon was over and became affectionate and smitten with each other. What do you expect from a

horny ex sailor? It wasn't too long before winter came that I moved to Brockton to be closer to her. I lived at the YMCA for a while and then met her parents. They lived in an apartment there in Brockton and seemed very nice. We got along great and before too long they invited me to move in and share a bedroom with her brother who was going to school to be a pharmacist. Her dad even got me a job at the Stop and Shop grocery store about two miles away. Once again, I had to walk to work through the snow both ways just to bag groceries and shag carts in the parking lot. At least there were sidewalks. Her mother said to me one morning as we sat and had breakfast that Sherrie and I should get married and start a life with children etc. Two days later, I packed and bid farewell and moved to the other end of town closer to the hot blonde that worked the register at the Stop and Shop. Debbie, very friendly, pretty, and silly just the way I like them. I got a job closer to where she lived and rented an apartment nearby. I started work at an old factory built in the 1800's that was four stories high and solid rock exterior with wood post and beam interior. Shoes were made their back in the day, as Brockton was the shoe capital of the world at one time in history. Me and my buddy Kenny H worked there and mixed cork for innersoles for shoes. We would open a 50-gallon drum of solid tar, break it into smaller pieces, and put chunks of it in the cauldron to melt it. Then we would put particles of cork into the wooden drum like a cement mixer and after, pouring measured amounts of tar into that. After cooling, we spread it into 12" x 12" wooden forms for shipping. Just Kenny, Mr. Bean, and me. Then the boxes were shipped off to Leavenworth Prison for the prisoners to work with and make inner soles for shoes. Bean was the supervisor at this giant facility from the past and was a great guy to work with. We would walk around after smoking some weed and explore this huge factory. Items were just left on the workbenches as if the place was told to vacate immediately. This place had carvings and names in the beams and columns. This was fascinating to me, I looked at all of them. Then one day, all operations came to a halt for us. We had been laid off. The building was shut down and not long after disassembled for the great salvage it supplied. Wood beams and flooring that would be used in residential work. I wish I had some of that.

I went down the road to another ancient facility that cleaned cowhides to make leather shoes with. Kenny moved on somewhere else. The hides were put in large wooden rotating drums, cleaned with a solution, then put on wooden flat carts and I would bring them to the drying room and hang them up overnight. The next morning, I took them down and brought them to another room for shipping. Boring, but I had to eat and buy weed. Then I got a new job, working at Franklin Auto Parts delivering parts to auto repair shops and Sears. This building was historic as it once was a place where they built buggies for people to have them pulled by horses. Many buildings like this in New England. Post and beam construction. Really old buildings and their construction was fascinating. They don't build places like that anymore.

I liked this new job because there was something different to due during the week. Deliver auto parts or stock shelves up in the attic with the names carved into the post and beams from 100 yrs. earlier. While I worked there, I would grab a sandwich at lunch and sunbathe on the loading dock out back. There was a parking lot behind the store where local workers would park and walk to their jobs in town. I went out there to try to talk to this beautiful young woman that passed by the shop every day. Everyone knew what time she went by, and we would all stare out the window at this image of beauty. Well one day I was sunbathing at the dock out back during lunch and she had left work early. I asked where she worked. This went on for a few days and to my surprise soon she was coming to the apartment for a visit. Just a visit. I was falling in love quickly and she gave me a framed picture of herself and said she had to return to Memphis in a few days as her mother became sick and needed her. I was heartbroken because we talked about marriage. When she left me and the boys at the store sure did miss her walking by. I did not see her again for years.

Kenny and Peter A and I got an apartment together about a half mile away from the auto parts store and this place was on the second floor and one bedroom. They didn't stay there all the time, but I did. Kenny and I would share the bed sometimes when there wasn't a girlfriend around because we only had one bed. (Don't even go there.) We got a minor bird and named him Maxwell. He would drink Boone's Farm

wine and chew on pot seeds when we gave it to him. We had steam radiators for heat and Maxwell would hiss like the radiators or say a few words like Boones Farm. There was a closet in the living room that was inhabited by pigeons. They came through the third-floor roof overhang and down the wall somehow. When we had a girl over, they all would ask what that noise was. Then we would open the closet door as if we didn't know and scream with them. Too funny.

There was a woman that lived in a building next door that was married to a firefighter. At night, when he was gone, she would open the shades and walk around naked and after a while of this girly show I returned the favor. I would get in the shower, come out with my shades open and stand there drying off while Kenny would look from another window to see if she was looking. She was. So, this became a regular thing. By now, my hair was getting long, and I was considered a hippy type. I rented a new apartment with my friend from work, Bob C. He was an Elvis Presley type with the hair and all, he was from the back country in Maine. Then he met my friends and he soon changed. I was known as big Bob, and he was little Bob. We got along great and rented a bigger place on Exchange St. nearby. This place was a drug emporium for friends and us. My friend from high school Tony P and his three friends formed a band, The Cockroach Blues Band and would practice all the time there. Little Bob would join in as rhythm on his guitar sometimes and all was good. One night we put a hit of orange sunshine (LSD) in a quart of Coke. Then we passed it around for a swig and smoked some weed. Little Bob started laughing so much we put him in the closet and then took a drive to the park. Saw many things that just were not there. Deer and other animals and such crossing the road. Came back to the apartment and Bob was still in the closet and when I opened it, he started laughing again. I had to switch jobs again and went to work for Auto Drive Away. I went into Boston to pick up and deliver a car or get a bus ticket to somewhere to bring one back to Boston as far away as D.C. then one cold day me and the band decided to take an Auto drive away car to Ft. Lauderdale Florida that came up for me to deliver. We went all the way to Dania Beach FL. A beach town south of Ft. Lauderdale and set up camp about a half mile down the beach away from everyone. The first night someone

had broken into the car and luggage rack and took everything. We only had what was on our backs and in our pockets. We made palm thatch huts, had a campfire pit on the beach and that went on for about 3 weeks. We went to the local Salvation Army and purchased used clothing and shoes. Three weeks later they headed back, and I stayed, just me the coconuts, and the sound of the surf. I started to look for a job. Found one at Red Lobster about a mile up the main road and worked in the kitchen washing dishes. They wanted to move me up to hush puppies and I said no thanks. After all, I was eating like a king. Some many lobsters, crab, steak never been touched. Yummy.

I went to a yoga society function and the yogi gave me a two-syllable mantra to practice meditation that I still use to this day. I moved on from the kitchen and got a job with two Lesbians. They had a tire recycling business and I drove a big truck to different tire shops, picked up used tires, and brought them to a recycling facility. One woman was a butch dyke and carried a pistol the other an ex married woman with an 8-yr. old boy. They invited me to live with them and I had to walk thru their bedroom and share a room with the kid. Strange stuff to me. I soon found a better job with a remodeling contractor Mr. Moon. We worked on different homes in the area doing general remodeling. I once was on this home by the river and the owners had three dogs. They would love to bark at the sunbathing alligators when one day I heard a yelp and a collie disappeared.

Then soon after my good friend from Brockton, Mike K came to visit and stayed a week or so and we decided to hitchhike all the way to Calif. To see a friend from Brockton that got into the movie business. He was playing a mortician apprentice with the late Olivia De Havilland. On the way out of Florida we scored some white cross pills. This is a form of speed. Later, some guy that just got back from Vietnam and was drinking beer picked us up, along with a longhaired guy he did not like. He pulled over, got more beer, got back in the car and pulled a pistol on this guy, and threatened to blow his brains out. When he stopped to pee, we all bailed out and hauled ass. Mike and I kept going and in Louisiana, we got another ride. This man picked us up and stopped in Baton Rouge and got a room with the intent he was bringing over a girl that liked sex with several men. We were as

giddy as kids at a carnival. Then he comes back, knocks, and Mike answered. All I heard was do you guys want to watch some porno. I said let him in. Mike turns around and said he wants to make a porno with us doing each other for 50 bucks. WHAT. Get the fuck out we said together. The next morning, we took two blankets and continued I-10 West into Texas. That night in Texas, we got a ride from a young blonde college girl, and we all got along great. She had to let us off at her exit near Austin and we couldn't hitch a ride and ended up on the side of the road sleeping under an old, abandoned truck. It was freezing and we had to make spoons and breathe on each other's face to stay warm. The next morning in the freezing drizzle, we tried again, and were picked up and drove for a few hours and we were let out in a desert area. No traffic at all for hours. At least it had warmed up some. Then we see a VW bus coming down the hill going in our direction. Holy shit it has Massachusetts plates and a couple of hippies in it. What a stroke of luck. Zoom, right by us like we didn't exist. Must have been carrying some drugs or something. Bastards. Finally got a ride back out to the main highway and hitched a ride with a Lt. in the Navy. He had a two seat TR6 (Triumph) pulling a small trailer with a motorcycle in it and going to San Diego. He was tired, so we took turns at the wheel and Mike, and I popped some more pills and one of us got stuffed behind the seats sideways. Nonstop to San Diego we drove, and he let us spend the night with him in his room at the base. From there we hitched up to L.A. and sunset strip, and as we were walking towards the strip, we passed a family out on the front steps of their apt. and we joined them for a few tokes along with a very young girl, their daughter. Never saw that before. We called Kenny R in Hollywood and soon was at his apt. More smoking and cocaine. Piles of the stuff. We spent the first n2ight walking the strip and exploring all this bizarre place had to offer. I remember standing on the corner when this woman got out of her Mercedes and asked where she could get a motorcycle headlamp that she showed me. I didn't know, I told her. She looked a little screwed up and as she left, she told me she was Karen Black. She was a movie actress of that time. Several movies. The next day we ran out of weed, went to the famous Tower Records store down a few blocks, and ordered an ounce. The clerk went in the

back and came out with it in a Tower Records bag and said 10 dollars please. Off we went to the apartment.

That evening we went to the famous Whiskey a Go-Go club up the block on Sunset Strip to watch Buddy Miles play the drums with his band. Standing room only, and after a while, I was being nudged by someone but didn't think much about it as the place was packed. Then a push and I turned to be looking down at Rod Stewart and his girlfriend trying to leave. That was cool. The next day we all were sitting at an outdoor café laughing. I started to laugh just as three men in suits walked by and they thought I was laughing at them. The big one came over to me.

"What are you laughing at punk with his hand in his jacket as if to reach for a pistol.

"Not you guys I said."

He left. Close one. We spent a few days there and started back, this time to Brockton.

On the way we were picked up in New Mexico by a couple of guys that just got out of the Army, and they were heading to Mississippi, and we all took turns driving. We were in Meridian Mississippi, and I was driving, and we all wanted to stop for food. Got off the highway and headed into town. At a stop sign, I looked both ways, no one there and turned left. A young girl came flying over the hill and hit us broadside. Caved in the right-side door of the car but no one hurt. The cops came and arrested me for the accident. I was put in the cop car, and everyone was supposed to follow him to the station. Along the way, he got a call about something and floored it with both cars from the accident following as I looked out the back window and watched as they tried to keep up. What a total screw up this turned out to be. At the police station, I was put in a cell and given a fine of $250. The Army guys paid the 25.00 bail and got me out pending court. We all hauled ass. Never did go back.

We were let out somewhere in Alabama, Mike wanted to head back to Brockton, and I decided to go back to Florida due to winter up north and very little house framing in the winter snow.

Well, I started hitching a ride in the backcountry one morning and the locals didn't take well to some hippy stinking up the county. They would throw beer cans and bottles etc. at me and if they missed, would turn around and do it again. Full cans sometimes, or coffee, or whatever they could find handy. Finally made it back to I- 10 and before long three hot Alabama girls coming from a Florida beach stopped to give me a ride. Dianne the driver said, do you want to come to Selma with us? I said why not. We all got along like hippy people do and smoked weed on the way.

Once there Dianne said she would drop me off in a cow pasture down the road from her family's estate to spend the night. Yes estate, as in plantation, and pick me up in the morning. I woke up at sunrise under a tree among a herd of cows eating grass and watching me sleep. So strange for a city boy. Dianne came along and picked me up in her 340ci. Plymouth Duster muscle car. Then off to Selma where I was introduced to a friend of hers that was in the Air Force nearby, and he had a head shop in downtown right on the river. He sold weed supplies, black lights, posters, water beds etc. he wanted me to run the place during the day as he was at the base most of the time. I stayed their full time and slept on a waterbed that was on display and sold the kids smoking paraphernalia when they got off the school bus. Mostly looky loos. Dianne would come by after community college classes and after hours, we would get down in the waterbed room. There was a band that would practice in the back room overlooking the river and a few times they showed me some cords on the base guitar to fill in when their base player was too screwed up to play and didn't show. This band turned out to be Wet Willie and made around five albums with some songs that went to the top ten back then. Well, I guess I was a substitute rock star of sorts, what a claim to fame almost. Come to find out they are making a comeback now.

Dianne soon got an apt. in town and had many druggie friends over, and one night they scored some heroin and shot it up for the first time.

I chose not to and watched them all act like doped up zombies. Glad I didn't try it and never did. One night Dianne let me have the hot rod as I called it and me and two friends went to a nightclub out of town to watch a guy (Charles L) we met from the back room of the store play electric guitar at this club. He was great. Said he grew up with Jimmy Hendricks. On the way out some black guy asked if we were going into Selma and needed a ride. I said OK, come on. On the way, we passed around a joint and he didn't want any of it. He did ask if I could stop at a phone booth so he could call his girlfriend and he would stay on the drive to Selma if she were not home. Here is where things went bad. On the way into Selma, we went over the famous Edmund Pettis Bridge. Yes, the one that Martin Luther King marched over with hundreds following to start civil rights and were arrested and had been beaten badly.

When we got to a 4-way intersection just over the bridge, police converged on all four sides. A cop stuck his head in the car, looked at me and said don't you know it's against the law to drive bare foot in Alabama. I said come on you didn't know I was barefoot. Ya'll get out of the car and hands on the hood. By now, the local TV station was there, reporter and all, filming this big-time event. Front-page news the next day. Radio big story as well. They searched the car and said they could not find anything. My friend had stuffed the small bag of weed in a coke can. Search it again the chief said. They found it and tossed it onto the hood of the car and spoke. Chief, marijuana. Book them the chief said with the reporter all excited and cameras rolling. Good thing they didn't know what windowpane acid was. It is translucent and thin like stretch wrap in small pieces, and it was scattered on the floor of the car.

Off to the poky again. Had my own cell for a while. There were many blacks as you could imagine being in a Selma jail, what I mean is with all the white black hating cops there in Selma. The city of Selma still had separate restrooms to separate us in the restaurants there. Then one time at the restaurant this older man said to the cashier, this place stinks as he turned to look at me. My two friends were bailed out right away by parents or relatives and I remained in for six days. They wouldn't let me wear my shoes, wash, brush my teeth or change my

clothes. I was a thorn in the side of society, a heathen, no count s.o.b drug-taking misfit to humanity. Then they put this escaped convict from Michigan in the cell with me.

"I asked him, what you in for with my best jailhouse lingo.

"MURDER he said"

I did not sleep that night and luckily, Dianne convinced her parents to bail me out. So here they come that evening her mother driving the station wagon, her father in the back on a stretcher (he was disabled for life and didn't get out much) I had to get in the back with him per his request, he said take a few hits of this moonshine son. You will feel better. When we got to the plantation (I didn't know where they were taking me) the night servant had a hot bath ready for me and said mister Robert, I have a bath for you, and I'll take your clothes and wash them. Here is a robe. Got my own bedroom too. The next morning, I was awakened by a different servant. "She asked if I would like some breakfast." Hell ya, I said to myself. No one else was up yet. So, her and I talked about stuff as we sat in the kitchen. Genuinely nice woman. I stayed a couple of days and noticed that the blacks that approached the house wouldn't even step on the porch. They stood back from the steps and spoke. Never see that up North.

Dianne decided she would go with me to Brockton and a friend of hers and mine drove us in his VW bus. On the way, we took turns with her in the back of the bus. This was the time of free love, remember. She liked it. Once there i got an apt for her and i. Started work for Jim Crann. He had a construction office around the corner. Talk about that in a bit. I worked for him on a storefront a block away and would walk back to the apt for lunch and she would have me for lunch. This lasted about 3 weeks and she got bored and somehow got a ticket back to Bama, never to be heard from again. It didn't take me long to find another. Linda D. Tall slim blonde with big hooters and smart as a tree stump. She was easy and loved me. Liked her a lot. Well, she claimed later that I got her pregnant, but she was screwing some other guy too. A little boy was born; John D and he did not resemble me a

bit. However, it was never proven. I still wonder. I still had my backup Debi, and she had a car.

I worked for Jim Crann as a carpenter and after the first week, he gave me a dollar raise. I did good work. He would take me on trips to the lumberyard and tell me about his experience in the Army as part of a top-secret company that was dropped in Germany behind enemy lines. He was taught German and when they parachuted in at night, they would change into street clothes and blend in with the enemy. This was known as the famous Wild Geese in WW2. There was a movie about this, and he told me that only him and one other had survived the ordeal and got out of country unharmed. He then went on and told me that after the war he and his army buddy decided they would rob a bank using the skills they were taught in the Army. That did not go over well, and he spent 13 yrs. in jail. He went on further with more stories and told me he was an ordained minister or warlock. A male witch. Jim was a single man if you haven't already figured it out. I was his friend, I guess. I got my buddy Kenny H a job with us, and Jim asked him if he knew anything about plumbing. Kenny said yes and he went over to his house. What Jim meant was his plumbing in his pants, said Kenny. They both drank and smoked weed then, Jim passed out and Kenny left. That's too funny.

I stayed with Jim on another job, government housing project. New ground up, with many buildings. Sometimes they had to blast rock out of the ground with a steel mat over the blast to stop it from scattering all over. I saw a boulder come out of the ground the size of a Volkswagen and it lifted the mat aside and crashed through the corner of a building. Wow. Cool.

Well winter was coming on again and I started to work for Kenny A. A person my age with a bad attitude. Four of us would meet at his place and drive into the job site. Mostly homes and apartment framing. I was strong as a bull and would carry 8-10 2x4 studs on my shoulder, up the stairs. Or two bundles of shingles (140 lbs.) up a ladder to the second-floor roof. We would do this during the warmer months and then work inside during colder months.

Somehow, I got hooked up with Mike's sister Meredith and started living at his mother's house with her and her two sisters. I would do work on the exterior of their home for room and board. Meredith and I would sleep on the pull-out couch most of the time. Alternatively, sometimes with her sister Andrea in her king bed. No fooling around allowed there. But she did ask a lot of questions about why guys are the way we are. I was honest about it and told her what she wanted to hear.

By the next spring, I moved into Kenny H parent's back yard in Bridgewater, Ma. They had a wooded area and I set up a tent and put plastic over it strung from branch to branch to stay dry. I had a three speed Raleigh bike that I made a tent for also and surrounded the place with a tree branch fence and a self-closing gate. Very cool place. I always had visitors come by my tent because it was so hippy like. A hovel of sorts. Always had some weed to share. I would pedal my bike a couple of miles away to a framing job on some condominiums with my tool belt around my waist. My friend Peter A would come by, always walking and would dress like David Carridean from the Kung Foo TV series. The hat, satchel, and long cane. Peter was always mellow and cautious, still the same today. One-night Peter and I went to Richard W's house (we called him snots), and he took us out for a ride in his old 1940 something Plymouth. Every time he hit a bump in the road the rear axle would slide out from one side, and we would have to stop and put the sledgehammer back under between something to keep it from doing it again. Then one night we went to his house for a smoking party. We would sit in a circle, pass around some weed, put the stubby end's (roach) into a wok, and let it smoke the whole place up. Peter and snots started fake sumo wrestling for everyone's amusement. We also dropped some acid to ramp up the high. I got too high and walked outside to get some air. I was looking at the stars and somehow walked out into the street and traffic. Horns started beeping and I jumped back and landed into a culvert. Then I went and sat down under a tree tripping heavy. A few minutes passed and looking at the road I saw a horse drawn hearse coming. As it went by, I saw a body in it, and it was mine. Holy shit that is definitely an omen. Later, that night we went in the car and came through the back fence of the local drive-in theater and saw Barbarella with Jane Fonda while sitting on

the hood. I never touched acid again. Just mescaline or some other forbidden drug.

After that job finished and winter was coming on, I moved back to Brockton. Tent life was getting a bit chilly. A friend, Ronny V and his dad hired me. Italians, and his dad was from the old country as well as the whole crew. We worked on building an addition to the Howard Johnson hotel in Boston. Peter and I decided to move there, and we got a small place on the famous Beacon Hill. Probably the oldest apartment buildings in the country. We had one room with a small kitchen and a bathroom door that you couldn't close if you sat on the pot. Very historic area. Sometime in 1974 one morning it was too cold for them to lay block and mortar, I was driving the high lift, and I had put a piece of plywood on the front of the forks and pushed the snow aside. Still was not at 32 degrees by noon and we all went to the theater next door and saw the movie The Exorcist. The old Italians bailed out before the end, called their wives, and said to get the kids out of school now. Mass panic with them as the Catholic's they were, and I didn't feel too good about it either.

Life on the hill was great, lots of young people and businesses that was our preferred style. If we needed to get across town, sometimes in the winter we would grab the back of a bumper, slide down the road on the ice or snow. On the other hand, take the subway. Cheers as in the TV show was right around the corner but it wasn't well known then. Lots of great places to visit and Boston is still my favorite city.

Chapter 7
On The Road Again

After that job had finished up Peter and I hooked up with Auto Drive Away and got a car to deliver to Phoenix. Winter was brutal and work was scarce as usual.

So off we go with a passenger that I don't remember and dropped him off along the way. We headed down to Texas and stopped in Dallas to see Kenny H who had moved there earlier. It was late at night when we arrived, and he was living in a small trailer and the door was unlocked. Peter went in, jumped on him After that job had finished up Peter and I hooked up with Auto Drive Away and got a car to deliver to Phoenix. Winter was brutal and work was scarce as usual. while he was asleep and scared the hell out of him. Peter and I left at daybreak and cruised on into Phoenix. We went to a friend of Peter's home, a girl he knew from someplace and stayed the evening with her and her parents and siblings and her mother had cooked some great Mexican food that I wasn't familiar with at the time, and I haven't stopped eating Mexican since. Anyway, the next day we got a furnished one-bedroom apt. in a very nice building. Peter of course slept on the couch and left the bedroom to me. In the morning we went looking for work and I headed west on Central Ave, and he went east, walking of course since we dropped off the car that morning. The walk from the apt. was great. We had date trees, orange, grapefruit trees that hung over the fences, and we would pick all we could eat. Peter found a job in a high-rise office building that had a nice restaurant in it. He worked in the kitchen etc. I found a job at Dell Web's Townhouse, an upscale hotel with a 5-star restaurant and I was working in the kitchen as well. They started me out getting food prepped for the 10 cooks and German chef along with about 10 other people that worked there.

After a few weeks, they moved me up to making ordure's on mirror trays; I had made a tray one day with coconut that I colored with different food colors to make a desert scene where the food looked like it was growing out of the tray. The German chef and guest where amazed and complimented on it. The Chef came to me and said I am giving you a dollar raise but do not tell anyone because I just don't do this. Next thing you know I'm making deserts as well as mirror tray orders. We all dressed in chef coats, checkered pants, and tall white caps and when I went downstairs to change in street clothes, I would put some food under my hat and walk down like a freaking runway model to balance the free food. One-day president Ford came there to talk about something in the grand ballroom. A week before he showed the fed's where there watching everything we did. The day before, I had made 2000 Jell-O deserts with a cherry and they followed me to the bathroom, and into the cooler, everywhere I went because I was handling food. The day he arrived was tight security and when he was making a speech, I went out to the loading docks and peeked into the ballroom, soon to be picked up under the arms by the secret service people and brought back to the kitchen. After my shift, I went out front, joined the hippy protesters, and smoked weed with them. Peter had met this girl named Katie. Now, I have never known Peter to be seen with a girl or guy and to this day, that still exists today.

Anyway, we three decided to share a house together not far from downtown and close to Central Ave. it was an older home in a quiet area 3-bedroom, 3 bath's, 3 porches with a garage for Katie's car. It also had a back yard and Katie planted veggies and things? On a side note, Katie's father was a federal judge and was in isolation at his condo because of the man that had killed and threatened other judges. That man is Woody Harrelson's father. You know, the actor. Anyway, we all liked to sit on the porch and get high. Oh, happy days. While I was at the kitchen job, the head chef invited me and Kenny H (he came for a visit) over to his house because he knew we liked to smoke. Larry L was his name and he asked us if we were interested in smuggling a hundred pounds of weed each in special backpacks across the border. He explained he drove a small bus full of it through a hole in the fence at the border. It was documented as the Nogales

hole. I saw the article wrote up in the paper he had kept. We would each get a thousand bucks. The day came to do this, and we went to his place, and he handed us the backpacks and each of us a 45-caliber pistol.

"What's this for Larry" He spoke

"In case the federales' start shooting at us."

The deal was off right then. I knew too much, and I got tired of the kitchen scene, as I am more of an outdoor type and got an offer to work as a carpenter again.

This time at the city of Scottsdale on an Olympic size swimming pool, building the forms for the concrete floors for the outbuildings around the pool. I thought winter was bad and this was just as bad with the heat at 100 plus degrees. We started at 6am and worked until 2pm straight thru. This was union pay scale and benefits. We also had to wear gloves all day to pick up the tools. We all got tanned except for our hands. That looked strange. After the day ended, the foreman would go by a case of beer, throw it in the pool, and we would all jump in and drink until all gone. The problem was I was up at 5am and had to walk 2 miles to hitch a ride with a fellow worker and walk back after work while carrying my tools This went on for weeks.

One day Katie asked me if I would ride along with her to visit a friend up near Bisbee AZ. This was a mining town in the mountains full of artist of many talents. We went down the mountain on the other side to her friend's location which was an artist's commune compound secluded away. They did lots of sculptures and paintings mostly. We spent a couple of nights there and Katie and I would share some blankets on the floor of this cabin that had a loft were her friend slept with her boyfriend. So, I'm half-asleep and then I feel Katie groping me, then it was on. I never did think of her that way and it never happened again. We never mentioned it either. I was asked if I would stay because they needed a carpenter. I came awfully close to saying yes. That would have been a life changer right there. I went back with Katie and my hot ass job in Scottsdale.

One Saturday night I hitched a ride to a nightclub I heard about with live music and peanut shells on the floor. I started talking to these two girls and one of them was a blonde-haired girl (smart as a tree stump again) named Carol. Very pretty. She brought me to her apt. that night and we took a bath together as per her request then she drove me home. Weird right? Soon after, we were a hot couple always together and did crazy stuff like jumping the fence to her elementary school she had attended and doing it on the slide. Or, jumping the fence to the drive-in theater because we didn't enough money to pay admission and sit on the ground and watch as she held my hands around her boobs in front of everyone there. One day she took me, Peter, and Kenny to the Verde River a hot spot for nudist and we all got naked and walked around with some people we did not know. One other night Carol took me to some mansion up on Camelback Mountain overlooking Phoenix were there was a party going on with some friends of hers. The place was crazy and come to find out the house belonged to Alice Cooper (rock star). Many people had makeup on like he wore, and I couldn't tell which one he was. I was very fucked up anyway to recognize much. Stuff like that was ongoing and I liked it. She was crazy though. And I liked it.

This was a time in life that is different as a hippie type. Like wearing sandals made from truck tires. Cool stuff then.

One day Katie brought me to a friend of hers place. They were just alike, flowery dresses and listened to Joni Mitchell all day. Her friend gave me a piece of peyote button and I went off on a trip like never before. I think I saw myself as a bird in my head, I was flying like a bird I thought. this was vastly different from the other stuff I had taken. I see why the Indians used it in their ceremony's. Very cool to be a bird or coyote.

About this time in my life, I had been in Phoenix for a year, Kenny and I were on the front porch smoking weed, and we had brought the TV out there to watch Saturday Night Live. It was in its first year then. Well Carol drove up and told Kenny and me that we were getting married in Sedona AZ and her parents were going to give us a thousand dollars and a trip to Las Vegas for a honeymoon. Wow! what shocking

news! Two days later I had packed my bags, booked a flight back to Boston, and had Debbie pick me up and bring me to her mother's apt. she was living at and slept on the living room floor with her. She started in on the marriage thing as well and I did not stay there long. I moved in with Mike's mother and sisters again but slept with Andrea upstairs, but we were just friends. No hanky panky. Andrea was only 20. Before long, I went to work with Kenny A again, but winter was coming on once more and work was scarce. He had cut my rate by two dollars per hour. Time to move on again.

Not long after that job was finished, I hooked up with Auto Driveway again and asked about anything going to Florida, as my whole family had relocated there a few years earlier. I drove a big Buick to St. Petersburg where they all lived at and delivered it. The couple whose car it was where nice enough to bring me to my brother Mike's house. Mike and Leslie had a small two-bedroom place near the Skyway Bridge spanning over Tampa Bay in St. Petersburg and I had my own room there. I didn't have a car, so I used my brothers van at night to go explore the area. After a while Mike got me introduced to this crane operator and his wife because they had a car they wanted to sell. A little yellow foreign something, but better than walking and I could make payments on it. Free at last. I scoped out the area and saw a house being remodeled and stopped and asked if they wanted the shingled roof replaced. Bingo. My first job. Before long I had hired my younger brother Jonathan as requested by my mother and got started. He was a pussy and didn't like that work. I made him do it anyway. I also had to help my father on his remodeling work, as I was the only carpenter in the family and for free. Why just me? Before too long my father got me a job with my two older brothers and him at the power plant they were building as boilermakers. My father was erection superintendent (what a title) I spent a couple of years there learning new skills as a union boilermaker, welding, burning steel, and fitting pipe. Great money as well. Bought myself a nice dodge van and started hanging out at a topless bar after work sometimes which was a new experience for me. Soon I got my own apartment near the bay, and I would run about five miles on the beach a lot after work or on the weekends. You know when I wasn't at the topless bar.

While there, my brother Mike and I were becoming friends with a carpenter at the power plant. He had made over 3000 skydiving jumps and got us interested. Soon we went to a sod farm that had a grass field for aircraft takeoff and landing. We went through a brief instruction and was headed to the Cessna, a 4-passenger plane. Mike wanted to go first, and Frank a guy from work wanted last. He was scared to death and started dry heaving as Mike, and I laughed. He was so macho at work. I jumped after Mike and climbed out on the wheel strut with one-foot dangling and holding the wing strut as instructed. Pushed off and the static line opened the shoot a couple of seconds later. What a thrill. I landed and got up to gather the shoot but soon fell as I tried to walk. Thought I had sprained my ankle. The next day it was swollen worse, and I stayed home to ice it down. The next morning, I drove to the hospital for it to be checked out. You have a broken ankle they said, how did you get here? I drove and hobbled in I said. Hobbled out with a cast up to my knee. Had to drive with my left foot. Two months later got the cast off and went back to work. Then went back to skydiving without incident for a few more jumps.

Soon I was introduced to a young woman named Joanne by the wife of the guy that sold me the car. She worked in the cosmetic department of a well-known store, and I didn't take to her right off because of all the makeup she wore. I was still into hippie chicks. She seemed very nice though. I got her phone number but waited around two weeks before I called. I think I took her to a miniature golf place on the first date. A few days later out to eat. Then this became a regular event. One day she invited me over for lunch or something and cooked. Her idea of a grilled cheese sandwich was two pieces of toast with a slice of cold cheese. Disgusting, but a sweet attempt anyway. On the other hand, sometimes a can of Campbell soup with it. So, I showed her how to make spaghetti, the right way. A box of pasta with a can of Ragu sauce over it. What a connoisseur I was. Anyway, we started seeing each other always and before long, she said we could move in together at her apartment. I was glad to get out of my brother's house since he and Leslie got divorced and he was a difficult person to deal with always. Things were going good with Joanne and I, and we went all over the area of St. Petersburg, the museums and of course the

beaches. My job wasn't going to last forever, and the day came for layoffs for many of us. Couldn't find any more work, so I packed my bags and headed off to Brockton again in my little green Nissan that I traded my van for. Once there I went back to work for Kenny A and started living with my friend little Bob and his girlfriend and two kids. Slept on the couch but I didn't like it there because his girlfriend was a big slob and left diapers on the coffee table and elsewhere. I got behind on my car payments and one morning it disappeared even though I was parked behind some tall hedges. Repo man got it. I was back to hitchhiking again and would catch a ride to the Cape and sometimes go to the nude beach. On a good weekend, there would be over 3000 people there including entire families. There was a park ranger since this was a national seashore and he would walk the beach with a see thru vest with his badge pinned on it and nothing else, how funny. One time hitching a ride there a guy picked me up and was headed to the same beach. Once there he taught me how to juggle balls. Three tennis balls (do not go there) and I practiced this and became fairly good with the juggling over time. Once little Bob drove us there and he was so excited about all the naked girls he had to lay on his belly. I was thankful for that. I didn't want to know Bob that way.

Well, the winter came on again and work got really slow, and I was living back at Mike's mother's house, but no girlfriend this time as Meredith had moved on. Mike called me there and said you need to come to Texas where all the work is. He had been living there for a year or so with his girlfriend Debbi, also from Brockton. So, I gathered up my things. A suitcase, my toolbox that Jim Crann gave me and 30 bucks in my pocket. Mike K was paying for the airfare and his mother drove me to the airport. I arrived at Hobby Airport early evening, and we went to his apartment in Pasadena. When I got out of the car I asked, what the hell was that smell. It was the nearby paper mill. Pasadena was a low rent area of Houston and very redneck at the time. Work was plentiful though and the next morning Mike drove me to a refinery that was being built in Deer Park nearby. I passed the physical exam and was to start the next morning at the Shell Oil Refinery under construction. Somehow, I hooked up with this guy Robert that was living in the same apartment complex, and he worked there as well.

We drove there and back each day for months. When I first started that winter there was a cold spell that was the worst in decades, around the teens. Most of the plant workers stayed home. I was wondering what happened, you know me being a hardened Yankee from the cold and all. The men that did stay huddled in plastic wind barriers with the welders to keep warm. I met many new friends there especially co-workers and our safety officer that would drive some of us to the pipe yard in the company truck and light up a joint. What a guy. One day our crew foreman, an older fellow joined us for lunch at our makeshift tent and asked if he could have a brownie, we all grabbed them and stuffed them in our faces. They were full of cannabis. What a buzz that was at work. Soon after saving up some cash, I ended up buying Mike's old Buick to get around in, but the following Monday the front wheel fell off on the way to work. Oh, shit. Got it fixed and life went on. One time we took the Buick (Mike called it the couch) to Galveston for a deep sea-fishing trip, and I got seasick. How could that happen, after what I went through in the Navy? Ended up getting my own apartment in the same building but i had no furniture. I took some stuff from the poolside, metal furniture and bought a mattress. I started going to this topless place nearby and got hooked up with this girl from New Zealand who was 6' 1" barefoot. We dated a couple of times, and she always wore heels that made her 6'4". Two inches over me, that was uncomfortable, and everyone would stare at her then look at me as to say what the hell did you get into.

I think I stayed at the plant for six months and then quit for an opportunity to frame homes for Deer Park Lumber. I would go to this little breakfast café every morning before work. This Mexican girl Alma was sweet on me as she brought my breakfast each time quickly. Got great service and I dated her a few times. She was a wild child. Anyhow, I started working for the lumberyard as they had started a home building company and the two brothers over saw this for their father. The one brother David would come by the job site in his Jaguar with smoke billowing out of it when he opened the door. He smoked lots of weed if you didn't guess by now. Me and Chris W who I had met earlier started this up and did all the framing and exterior trim work ourselves. Chris was a carpenter from Michigan who I met at the

apartments. We had framed many homes for this company over a year or so span. Between that job, we worked for a person named Robert E. He was a home framer and was quite impressed with our quality, speed, and skill level. We were making around the same money subcontracting or working by the hour. We liked the weekly paycheck better. He also was from Deer Park and got me involved with this country bumpkin named Wadeen. She was all-Texan and never dated a Yankee before. Robert, our two girlfriends and I went to a few events like the horse track or a pub. All four of us in the front seat of his truck. Squish. They never hung out with a Yankee before either. The time we went to the horse track, they were all dressed country style and I came out of my room looking like a city slicker, they just stared at me in disbelief.

Not too long after the Buick got old, I bought a 69 Mercury Cougar. This car had a lot of horsepower and would burn rubber in three gears. Chris and I would drive it to work because he had wrecked his 240 Z car when he came down from Michigan. The boy had a drinking problem. I started thinking about Joanne again and how I missed her. I called her several times only to be hung up on. Finally, we talked, and she said she would come to visit.

I picked her up at the airport and before we got out of the gates we had made up. That was a major turn on and when we got to my place, the clothes came off. I was smitten and so happy to see her we talked some more that night. She decided that she wanted to move here and be with me under the assumption we would get married, I was thrilled at the idea. I flew to Tampa soon after and she picked me up at the airport and we went to her apartment. The next day she had quit college and we rented a small, enclosed trailer to pull with her little Chevy Chevette and headed back to Houston. We stayed at my apartment until we found an apartment in South Houston along the freeway. Brand new and it had never been lived in. At this point in life, I had found a job on Nasa Road 1 at an upscale townhome project on Clear Lake doing punch out. Didn't even know what that was then. I learned quickly and stayed on for about a year and a half. I bought a 73 Grand Prix from a co-worker for $400.00 it was in perfect condition and ran like a bat out of hell. This job became boring sometimes and

we would throw wood or Styrofoam in the water and shoot it with our nail guns for entertainment. Or fly kites off the rooftops. Then one day a new supervisor came along, Burt. He was from Jersey and what a dick he was. We butted heads often especially when my daughter was going to be born. He said I had three children and worked every time one was born. I told him to fuck off, I'm going to the hospital. We never did see eye to eye.

Chapter 8
Time To Settle Down

One day about six months after Joanne being here, we decided to get married. So, I arranged a wedding at Mike and Debbi's house with all my rowdy friends present. I bought two gold bands at a pawnshop and hired a black judge as he was 50 bucks cheaper than the white judge was. (That person is a congressional representative these days) and had the wedding in the house and had a party. Joanne looked so pretty in her new dress and me in a suit I rented. I was still going through my bushy hairstyle at this time, no more hippy look since Massachusetts. It was soon after that Nichole was born in Galveston at John Sealy Hospital. This was a hospital for people who could not afford insurance, you could make payments. When we arrived at the hospital, they checked out Joanne and said she was not ready yet and to come back later that day. Off to the seawall we went and parked along the Gulf, and I watched the surfers as Joanne lay in the backseat moaning. When she could not handle the pain anymore, we went back, and they admitted her finally. A few hours later, I was invited in to watch the delivery and when the baby came out, they put her in my arms, and I started to cry. What a joy this was and still is today.

I was finally laid off from the townhome project as it was near completion and a new friend, Wayne that I had met there told me about a condominium project on El Dorado Blvd that needed punch out help. I applied and was hired on right away. I met this weird guy named Bobby S. from NYC and we worked together for several months and became close friends. His father as it turns out was the lead NYP detective on the Serpico case. There was a movie made about this. A new condominium project with the same company was started right next door and I was promoted to supervisor of punch-out and designed

and built all the wood decks around the pools. I saw some strange things in some of the units such as pounds of weed under a bed or the girl that took naked pictures of herself in the mirror and left them on the counter. I took the liberty to pick up her Polaroid camera and take a pic of myself, naked of course, and left it on the counter next to hers. I thought that as so funny. Then there was a single man, Richard H that had a restaurant in Houston. His restaurant was called Dick Heads. How sick is that. As soon as some of the condominium's had been built, my boss Elsyne, a woman and Dan H the superintendent. Promoted me again to Asst. Superintendent. Now I had some authority but not without their permission.

The man that owned the General Contracting (Gene) company would come and we would go in his Bell Ranger helicopter and sometimes pick up some of us guys to go to another project across the city with our tools and all. Then fly us back with complimentary wine. What a deal that was. One time we went to work on his gigantic new house still under construction, and his pool had lifted out of the ground like a boat. About two feet, because it wasn't filled with water yet and we had several days of heavy rain. Never saw that before either.

One day we decided to move closer to my work and ended up in another apartment in Clear Lake. Joanne stayed home to raise Nichole and I worked six days a week. On her way back home from shopping one day she pulled into the complex and a huge tree limb came down on her car, crushed the roof, and collapsed the windshield on the both of them. Joanne was pinned in her seat and Nichole had glass all over her. A tree service company was responsible and had cut the limb with no guards or barrier. We sued and won a small sum of $3000. Joanne to this day has neck pain sometimes. Soon after Nichole turned two and a half I think and said her first sentence. We had a cockatiel bird, and it would fly loose sometimes, and it landed on her cup and would drink some. Smokie eats juice she said. Her first sentence. We were so surprised by this.

About this time in life, I bought a used Ford pickup from my friend Wayne. Great condition looked good and was a step up from the station wagon I had bought while at the condo job. I had to sell the Pontiac

as I needed cash. During this time, I was invited to start a bowling team with some co-workers, and we would practice sometimes during lunch break at the alley nearby. We started on a league at night, and we were doing well at it. There was one night during competition that I walked into the restroom and stepped on some kid's gum. When I got up to bowl, my foot got stuck and I went three big giant steps down the alley with the ball and landed on my ass. So fuckin funny they all thought. Then my truck was stolen from the apartment, and I got the insurance money, applied for a loan, and bought a brand-new Ford pickup. Had custom wheels put on this. What a fine truck this was. Then that was stolen with about 1500 miles on it. I was at Home Depot and had a cart full of lumber to bring back to a remodeling job I landed. A fellow contractor saw me pitching a fit and we loaded up his truck with my lumber and took it to the job. Genuinely nice gesture on his end. Then someone smashed the windshield on Joanne's car at the apartments. Time to move.

We rented a house in League City and then bought one soon after in the same neighborhood. 1200 sq. ft. for $63000. We were proud. I added on about 600 sq ft more with a beautiful, covered patio and separate dining room and extended the living room about 12 ft. We stayed there for about 12 yrs. This house backed up to a small airport that people would skydive at. Hmmm. Back in the sky again I was. I made 6 jumps there and had two malfunctions. Total of 10 jumps altogether and the situation was obvious. Quit while still alive. No more jumping out of perfectly good airplanes.

I think on my 40th birthday Joanne surprised me with a flying lesson at Ellington Field nearby. So, I show up and there is not a soul around. I figured that I would be in a classroom with others. So, I yelled out, hello, and here comes the instructor and asked are you, Robert? Yes I said.

He slides some keys over the counter and said let's go. We walk out to the runway and climb into a bottom wing four seated aircraft. With me in the pilot seat. Hmmm. He taxis out to the runway and tells me to push the controls to the firewall, go easy on the pedals to steer and I'll tell you when to pull back on the yoke. Gently pull back he instructs.

I pull back and off we go into the wild blue yonder just like the Sky King show back in the 60's.

He asked where I wanted to go. Over the bay I said.

This was very cool I thought. It was time to turn back, and he said bank left. I got too vigorous and put it into a steep bank, I was looking at the ground and he said that is enough. When we approached the runway, he said less speed and keep the nose up. I'm thinking, I hope he doesn't want me to land this. Then about 100' above the runway he said I got it from here. Wow.

Nichole went through school in the same district until graduation, this was the objective, to stay put for once. She was a very shy girl as a child, did not associate with anyone much and barely said hi unless we prompted her too. Well, that all changed with 9th grade and the boys and girlfriends at school.

She grew up fast, reached 6ft, and started to play basketball on the school team. However, like me she couldn't dribble down her chin. Chip off the old block they say. Joanne in the meanwhile started to work with NASA and has had some interesting space shuttle involvement over the years. Still works there to this day.

I started hanging out at the Beer Garden near the Space Center and met many astronauts and shot pool or played shuffleboard with them. They liked there beer as well. I then built a horseshoe pit and played into the night many times. I won a match one night against a train engineer, he had bet me a train ride if I had won. I did, so we walk across the street to a locomotive, and he starts it up. Off we go choo choo with me at the controls across two towns and catch another engine back to the Beer Garden. I mentioned this to Joanne the next day and she bit my head off. What if the cops stopped you? How would they do that? I smartly said. When you stopped you freaking idiot?

I made lots of new friends there and one of them was Don W. I became son number 3 in his mind, and we drank, hunted, and fished together often. Then he got me into the Masonic Lodge around 1986 and I went through the teachings and the 3 degrees. All this is done

by word of mouth from a fellow lodge brother. None of it written and after a year I became a Master Mason. All of this comes from the original Mason's that hand carved the stone for cathedrals and similar stone structures across Europe in that era. They recognized each other by certain handshakes and words still used today. I'm proud to be part of the culture being a builder myself. Oldest fraternity in the world and still strong.

I left my job as asst. superintendent when it slowed down and tried my hand as a handyman as I was always a hands-on man and not a paper pusher. I put out fliers all over the area. That failed, so I found a job framing a building for a contractor named Ray H. This is when Kenny A came down from Massachusetts to get past the winter months with a carpenter friend of his named Mark C. We all worked on this building and then moved on to a Wendy's after. Soon after, we went to College Station, TX to work on a new McDonalds when Ray decided he couldn't make any money at this and gave up. Well, the general contractor (Gene S) asked if I wanted to finish the job with the people I had and said he would make sure that I did not lose any money doing this.

I gave it a go and it worked out fair. I had bought a small-enclosed trailer for tools, ladders and other things needed for the jobs. They were all cookie cutter versions for the most part and we always had what was needed. No get rich job but I was in charge again and felt like I hit a good position to be in. I must have built or remodeled 50 or more of those over the years with this contractor and there are too many stories to get into right now. That general contractor was one of the toughest people to work for I ever knew. He had been a major in the Air Force flying missions over Viet Nam at one time. I hated him but respected him as well. On a personal level, he was a great person. Gene would always wear a straw cowboy hat and when he got mad which was often, he would throw it on the ground and stomp on it. One night on a Red Lobster remodel he got mad at me and said, let's take this outside. I looked angry at him and said you don't want to do this Gene. He kept quiet and never said that again. Between those jobs, we did other projects for different contractors and kept busy.

71

Chapter 9
A New Opportunity

On day as I was working helping a millwork subcontractor (high-end woodwork) on finishing a nightclub called the Ocean Club in Houston he asked if I wanted to work on building a DJ booth at another new club? Sure. Mark and I worked on that, and this is where I met Allen C. A superintendent for McFadden Venture's, they were the largest owner of night clubs in the world. About 200 of them. His office was in Houston, and we worked on several clubs all over the country with Allen. Daytona Beach always comes to mind. I hooked up the trailer, loaded up two other guys, and drove there. The Daytona 500 was scheduled in a few days, and we couldn't find a parking spot anywhere at the hotel I booked. Then a stroke of luck, a parking spot. I parked the truck in it after we had dropped off the trailer at the job site. Well before long a knock on the door and guess who was there. Bill Elliot the #9 car driver for Budweiser. You are in my spot. So, we moved about a half mile away before we found a spot and walked back. The club we were going to remodel was three stories and directly on the beach, I mean the back patio was on the sand. You could drive on the beach for miles and check out the parties and bikinis forever. And of course, we did.

Allen never got the right permits to remodel, and we were shut down for a few days after the cops came and threatened to throw him in jail. The good thing was the Budweiser rep came by and gave Allen and I two pit passes to the Daytona 500. They wouldn't let you drink while in the pit, so we loaded up beers in our pockets and watched from the fence then went in with the action after a couple of cold ones. Very cool to say the least.

Then spring break came along, and the college crowd was wild. So wild that vehicles were getting broken into all the time, so I called my Uncle Edmond who had moved to St. Augustine Florida a few years ago about an hour drive north and stayed with them for 10 days and just made the drive every day. Some of the McFadden sound, light and video people came out and these people would work late at night and smoke weed into the wee hours hooking things up. We always had great music playing but very loud. I had around 13 men working on this club. A lot of them local. Bike week with bikers from all over the country came to show off their bikes and have a great time on the beach. You would think big trouble, but not one arrest was made the whole week. The only trouble was with the spring break crowds. Mostly college people blowing off steam. This job was when a carpenter of mine came up on the roof and threatened to throw me off for talking down to him. He was always a difficult employee and he amped up my stress level. We traveled all over the country remodeling these clubs for about 3 or 4 years. We had built knockdown stages for some of the best entertainers of the time and some elegant and not so elegant drink and drown type clubs. Tampa Bay comes to mind. The Ocean Club was a full-blown remodel and at that time, I had been having some issues with panic attacks from stress. I had one employee that always pushed my buttons, the same guy, and this did not help my stress at all. So, one day I had to leave the job and go to my hotel room as I was having a bad panic attack. I never had to leave work because of it before. I went to my room and flopped around on the bed like a fish out of water. I wanted to call an ambulance or the front desk but became too paranoid to try it. Totally disillusioned and incoherent I thought about jumping off my 4-story balcony to the pavement below. I went out there and cried then went back in. That night Allen took me to see the movie Full Metal Jacket. That didn't help at all. When I got back home to Texas, I went to a stress councilor three times to figure out my problem. After heavy medication and counseling we concluded that it was because of that one employee being so difficult to manage. So, I fired him, and my stress slowly disappeared. Nothing bothers me much anymore as I was at the peak of anxiety and will not let it happen again. Stress rolls off my back like water on a duck's ass.

The vice president of McFadden Gary C and Allen teamed up after McFadden Ventures collapsed and they started a general contracting business with hotels in mind. This is when my company Western Woodworks went into high gear. The first one was a Sheraton Hotel remodel in Houston that took 8 months. I was just a small business then and had to learn to grow fast. One other hotel comes to mind. The Marriott Grand Marquis, in Kansas City, Missouri. This is a heavy union city, and they didn't like scabs like us as they called anyone not union. We were on the first floor remodeling the night club and had a clear view outside with all the windows that wrapped around the corner of the building. We would see the guy that carried a picket sign all day saying we were nonunion workers. His name was Tony and we talked, and I brought him cold drinks time to time because of the heat as we sat on the low planter wall outside and talked. Then his business agent came along (in the black Cadillac) of course and said Tony why are you talking with him. He said Robert is a nice enough guy, we are just on different sides of the fence. So, I invited this man in for a look and he checked out the quality and he said, this looks good but don't ever try this in St. Louis or they will put cement shoes on you. A few days went by, and a couple of goons came looking for me. Came right up to me and asked where Robert is. Robert, I said with a confused look, well he stays in Houston I said nervously. Tell him we wanted to speak with him, and they left.

On another note, the mom and daughter performers The Judd's tour bus pulled up in front of the hotel and I watched as they got off. After a while, Naomi Judd appeared outside to walk her dog. Opportunity was knocking. I went outside and her and I talked for ten minutes or so alone as we sat on the edge of a low wall. More beautiful in person than on TV. Then Wynonna Judd came out with her bodyguard and unloaded two mountain bikes from the bus. They started across the 4-lane street, and he fell over in the road. What a du-fuss I thought.

I also had two hotel jobs in New Jersey at another time where I had to hire union carpenters to supplement my crew to avoid the same situation. It went well and they were great guys. Even sharing the leftover dinners with us when the wife made too much.

We also worked on the Hotel Galvez in Galveston, TX, which was built in the late 1800's, upgrading the lobby areas with pieces of old bars etc. from their warehouses. This was a job where I could express my design intent with the architect on what could or not be done with the old pieces. Still in place today. Made front-page news. Along the way, I was involved in five architectural awards, as I had worked on car dealerships, schools, airports, and courthouses. I have worked all over the country, east, west, Hawaii, Monterrey Mexico.

One time we had a hotel remodel in Sonoma California, wine country, where the white robe people stayed at. Aka the Hollywood types. One of the buildings was shut down that we stayed in and worked on. This was a three-story building and we had rooms on the second floor. Wayne and I shared a room. Well one-night Wayne woke up and woke me up and said he heard noises, I didn't. Then he woke me up and said someone was sitting on the corner of his bed, he pointed to the butt impression and, i saw this clearly.

Then it disappeared as if it got up and left. I said make a noise or something I'm not afraid of you. Then I heard the noise on the floor above us. This sounded like a party with music, laughing and glasses clinking. I looked at Wayne and said let's go up there. I'm not going up there he yelled. Just like in the movie The Shinning with Jack Nicholson. So, I went by myself. When I knocked on the door the noise stopped. I called the front desk, and they told me that's just our ghost's. They are well known here. Cool stuff I thought.

It was around this time one year that I had a stomach pain and Joanne took me to the hospital. They put me in a wheelchair as we checked in. I said I had to use the restroom and wheeled to it. I sat on the toilet and passed out, came to about five minutes later with my head slumped against the stall. What the hell happened I thought and knew I had to get out of there. I could only slide against the wall as I wasn't able to walk upright and went out in the corridor totally confused. I heard my name and I fell into the wheelchair. All I remember was going a hundred miles an hour down the hall. Then I felt people pulling me up on a gurney. They started pumping my chest and hooking me up and I slowly left my body. I hovered and turned over watching them

work on me and saw my wife nearby. Then I left and went upright into a tunnel of light. I saw people in the light that had died previously, some that I knew; I think one of them was my grandmother. This was the most peaceful, calm and stress less time of my entire existence. Or nonexistence in this case. Nothing could match the serenity. Finally made it to heaven I thought. Then I felt hands pushing me back down. I hovered over my body again for a moment and awoke to see them pumping on my chest and. I was angry. Please let me go back I thought.

I couldn't talk for a few hours coherently but found out later that my appendix had twisted and cut off the blood flow. I was saved again, just not my time to go yet. I recovered and continued with my travels.

I outgrew my rental shop and bought 1 acre on Louisiana Street in League City. This was a dirt road with a few homes and no water or sewer. I had to put in a well and septic system. I built a 3000 sq ft barn looking structure towards the back and nobody could tell if I had horses or what in there as many people had horses around the area. Joanne couldn't understand why I built a shop before the house. Hmmm she would say. Then I built the house, and she couldn't understand why it was a little smaller than the shop. Hmmm? According to the building inspector, this was the best-built house in town. He even had the other inspectors come by for a look at how wood framing should be built and take pictures. Cabinet quality framing I would boast.

It was about this time that a granddaughter came into our life. Her name is Summer. A beautiful blonde headed, blue-eyed girl. Nichole was married to a smart web site developer that had his own business. As Summer grew, she loved to pull her dog around in a baby carriage on the long driveway. Or play bad mitten with me and fly a kite or play catch. She is still somewhat of a tomboy today. I love her so much. She still is my favorite person in the whole world. Before too long I outgrew the shop behind my house with all the trucks, trailers and equipment and started looking for land somewhere not too far away. A friend of mine Shawn H who also was in the cabinet building business thought about doing the same thing as his rental shop leaked and was too small for his business as well. We ended up buying 8 acres together and split it down the middle. The next two years I drew

up a floor plan and layout of where it would sit on the land and how the machinery would lay out so the forklift could drive between most of the equipment. It finally happened and I built the greatest offices for myself and office personal upstairs. My office had a TV, lounge chair, private bathroom that was behind the bookshelf that opened a secret way. The business grew again with the bigger space, and I had to hire a truck driver and secretary. She also had a private bathroom and a draftsman along with a few more people to fill the overload of work. On the main floor were a restroom and a break room with a kitchen for employees. Things were going great then. I even laid out a future strip center to be located at the road in front, as my building was about 200 yards back. Had enough room for a baseball park behind it. Hmmm. I was the biggest business in town and the mayor presented me with a plaque at opening ceremony. He would drop by occasionally to see how things are. He loved to come by and watch the work in progress.

Sometimes, I would drive the truck and pull the trailer myself just to get away from the office. Usually by myself as I liked being alone for a couple of days. I would fly my people to the city we would work in, at a huge expense and sometimes have to rent several rooms $$$. Did I ever run up credit card bills! Occasionally the hotel that we were working in would put us up there. Some of these places went for $300 per night and they would let us eat in the employee cafeteria. These guys were getting a food per diem and would always eat all meals in the cafeteria when it was allowed to my disgruntle, but that was the company policy. After all, I was the one who created the policy. I should have included a clause. What a dummy.

One year my two nephews came down from Connecticut for the summer and worked with us. Scott and Ben. Two strong and eager young men that were on a break from school studying to be Architects. I took them on the road with me and the truck and trailer in tow. Once to Laredo Tx. The hotel LA Posada was right on the Rio Grande across from Mexico. While we were there Jennifer Lopez came to stay at the hotel, I waved and yelled out, but she ignored my presence. Bitch. I walked them over the bridge, which was a block away. We walked around town to explore the differences this town had to offer. They seemed very nervous and cautious, so we did not stay long. Then once

to Savannah Georgia, at a hotel on the river in the old section of town with the granite streets and buildings, from the ships that brought trade goods in from Europe and left their ballast behind. They were amazed at how polite people are there. On the way back we went through Florida and the beach towns and stopped for a swim near Pensacola. We took turns getting our trunks on in the 32' trailer we pulled and spent a couple of hours in the surf.

Life was good but the money I tried to collect was always out there in between their bank and mine, and not in my pocket. I couldn't save enough to put some back because the company was still growing. There were times I just didn't pay myself if things were financially tight. The employees, mortgage and credit card bills came first. At one point the 12,000 sq. ft. shop started getting small and I drew up plans to add 5000 more to the back of the building, and more equipment and floor space for the guys that needed more elbow room. Hotel remodeling was always needed in times of economic growth and my philosophy was get it while you can as I tried to instill in my employees.

In 2009, things started to slow down because of the economy crisis. Wall Street was taking a hit because of the subprime lending bill that Clinton passed a few years earlier. This gave homebuyers a chance to purchase a new home that they couldn't normally afford. Good idea gone bad. Millions defaulted on their mortgages and that is what sent the economy into a tailspin. Banks stopped lending money, even to the big corporations like the hospitality industry i.e., hotel owners. Allen's business was primarily hotels and shit rolls downhill i.e., me. I had to lay off 2 or 3 men but kept most on including my secretary to the bitter end being the optimistic type I was. I used up all the financial resources and finally had to shut down. I had to sell everything for 10 cents on the dollar and lost a small fortune. This is still a big sore spot in my heart today. I became the town drunk for a while as I hated the prospect of working for someone else after 28 years on my own.

Then things got financially worse, and we had to sell our home as well. Yes, the one I built. Got a butt load of money for it and purchased a home in the new subdivision Tuscan Lake. I had complained about this as they were removing acres of trees across the road from me.

78

Paid cash for the new house and I still live there today. Started to collect unemployment for the first time in my life. That helped a lot. Finally pulled my head out of my ass and went to school to become a catastrophe insurance adjuster. A man in my class called me and asked if I would go to Omaha to work as they have the worst hailstorms in the country and lots of roof work that needed to be estimated and repaired.

Off I went. Stopped along the way to visit my friend Ken H in Colorado Springs. He has a horse ranch just outside of Colorado Springs that I have been to before and he would always take me for a tour of Colorado, sometimes on horseback. What a life he has. Any way I was sent to Omaha from Cheyenne and that took 8 hours across Nebraska. The whole state is covered with corn as far as you can see. Cornhusker football, go figure. Once there I met my new boss, and he was starting up a company there to estimate and repair roofs. My job was to take measurements and write up a contract to the homeowner. At least try to get them to sign but I am not a pushy salesperson. One thing that stuck out was all the squirrels there and they had black fur. Anyway, he sent for his brother to work with me, and this guy was a total loser. He did not have a vehicle, I had to buy cigarettes and lunch for him until he was paid. If we pulled up at a red light and there was a girl next to us, he would roll down the window and flail his arms and whistle or yell out. How embarrassing this jerk was. I stayed for about six weeks and didn't do well financially. The office he rented was full of his family they were equally as stupid, or drunk or high on something. Then one night I heard on the news to beware of out-of-town license plates as these people will take your money and run, the news reporters said. Then I realized this is whom I'm working for. A sophisticated bunch of gypsies. I got a Nebraska corn huskers license plate frame to mask the Texas plates and didn't stay to long after that.

Chapter 10
Getting Too Old for This

Back to Texas I went broke, and out of work again. Disgruntled that I wasted my time with these people. Back at home, I got a call to be one of three superintendents at a time-share resort in Galveston, Tx for a few months. As needed basis. They worked me 7 days a week for three months, then laid me off.

Put out an add as a handyman in my community, which worked well when I worked. Then my friend Allen C called and asked if I could help on a 26 story Doubletree Hotel in Houston as one of the superintendents. I worked there about 7 days a week for 4 months, but they let me stay in a three-room suite with balcony. NICE. Back to handyman status after that. Then I got a call from a General Contractor in San Antonio. They needed a superintendent for a new LaQuinta, 4th generation hotel. I went there for 7 months, got laid off when completed because they didn't have any more work and didn't want to build hotels anymore. I liked it there and wanted to come back. Really good Mexican food. I purchased a Harley Davidson there, my third one, and wanted to ride the famous hill country roads. The month I had it while there I only rode it for 5 miles because I worked 7 days a week again. I liked that job because it was all mine. Just me, and I could take time for dropping off my laundry or grocery shopping and watching football on Sundays sometimes. I liked the hills compared to Houston flatness. One day in August I worked outside for hours unloading a semi-truck and sweated my ass off and had to go sit in the air conditioning of my office trailer. I had nearly passed out and I knew something was wrong and I drove to the hospital. I had severe heat exhaustion and one of my kidneys was failing from it. Spent 3

days there then drove home for a rest. Back at the job and towards the end of it.

I experienced another ghostly phenomenon. I was always the first one there in the morning and had to unlock the doors each morning. I would unlock the door at the end of the corridor and walk down the corridor to the sliding front doors to unlock them. Just as I reached for the latch I would here a metal and glass door slam hard down the hall. They were self-closing. It wasn't the one a came through as I would prop that one open each morning. This happened each morning for around two weeks. No reason for this noise at all. It wasn't windy. Then as I walked across the lobby I would here heavy footsteps going down the corridor above me. At this point I started to talk to whatever was there. I'm not afraid of you and you need to make another noise to verify you are here. Then I would go up to the second floor to look and it would stop. Nothing. I was hoping to connect with something. I told many people about this and explained that I think this hotel is on Indian burial ground as the Indians bury their dead-on high ground. This was the highest point in the area and the spirits were restless because they got covered over. I got a lot of strange looks or laughter. Little did they know about this?

So, here I am again working as a construction superintendent. This is a huge company and I'm one of about 45 superintendents. I am building a new building on the side of an existing one at the local mall. It takes me 10 minutes to get to work. What a deal. Who knows where I will end up after this? I'm 65 years old now and medical issues are coming at me left and right. Glasses to watch TV, hearing aids because of over 40 years of construction noise. Still, issues with my diabetes. Heart pumping issues. (Arterial fibrillation) numbness in my toes. Diabetic neuropathy. I refuse to acknowledge old age. I'm still going on 39 in my head until I look in the mirror. Oh, shit. So, I try not to do that. I have this sense of mortality and know I'm not one of those people that will live past there 70's. You know with the diabetes; blood pressure and A fib issues. I don't stress about this as stress rolls off my back like water on a duck's ass.

Chapter 11
Final Thoughts

Now that most of my craziness or irrational behavior is behind me and I live a normal life like most people. It certainly didn't start off that way and I thank the lord for the way I finally became who I am these days. There were many roadblocks for all of us and some never had the opportunity to change like I did. Lots of us run to the end of the chain and bark. Others break loose and lead better lives. I think I was one of those people. I did not grow up where there are white picket fences but most of us didn't either.

How big you want the desire to dream great things is probably equal to the desire to work hard and get ahead in life. Another thing in life is that it is important not to be power hungry, instead be a communicator and leave your mark as footprints in the sand so others can follow your lead.

Remember, it is better to die on your feet than to live on your knees. Try to do your best in life and the front doors will open for you. I hope you enjoyed my Obscure Life story as much as I did writing it.

Thank You All

Robert Forge

An Obscure Life
An Autobiography

Also, by writing this it has become a therapeutic tool for myself to step back and reflect on the struggles and triumphs in my life and, overcome and deal with the bad within. The book's title can be used as a verb or adjective. I use it as an adjective as in vague or unknown. So please do not judge me harshly and enjoy the story of

An Obscure Life.

I was shipped by bus from the recruiting office one day to the Navy shipyard in Philadelphia, sworn in with many others, and made some friends right off. After that, we were brought to a train station and put on sleeper cars for the long trip to Chicago. Once there we were put on a bus to Great Lakes Naval Training Facility just north of Chicago. Upon arrival, there was our company commander waiting for us and we piled out like a bunch of misfits.

robertforge70@gmail.com